Managing For Productivity In Data Processing

Written by:
JAMES R. JOHNSON

Q.E.D. Information Sciences, Inc.
Wellesley, Massachusetts

Published by:
Q.E.D. Information Sciences, Inc.
P.O. Box 181
170 Linden Street
Wellesley, MA 02181

Printed in the United States of America

Published by
Q.E.D. Information Sciences, Inc.
P.O. Box 181
Q.E.D. Plaza
Wellesley, MA 02181
Printed in the United States of America

Preface

It is interesting to note that ninety percent of productivity discussions emanate from the question "Why isn't Johnny coding?" But productivity is an all-encompassing topic, and individual productivity is only one of five productivity concerns in Data Processing. As a matter of fact, applying a generalized method of quantifying productivity may be more difficult at the programmer level than at other levels of responsibility within Data Processing.

Thus, this book addresses five aspects of Data Processing productivity in five parts:

    I.   Individual Productivity

    II.   Project Development Productivity

    III. Maintenance Productivity

    IV. Data Processing Division Productivity

    V.   Data Processing Corporate Productivity

An introductory explanation precedes each part. The book is based on experiences in a large state-of-the-art DP environment. It results from pragmatic experience--doing something wrong, and then modifying the approach and trying again. In some cases, the ideas may not seem sophisticated, but simple solutions are not always obvious.

Productivity issues cover a vast scope. Topics included have presented special challenges to the author. Few basic definitions are included. The only theory presented is found in Chapter Ten, which presents an "ideal" version of management training. The book deals with management issues, and assumes the reader is well versed in DP technology. The techniques advocated are pragmatic in nature and will improve productivity.

In order to introduce the material, selected questions from various chapters will be stated. If the reader is not interested in the concepts relating to the question, then the text is not recommended; conversely, if the question stimulates thought, then the chapters will provide insight into the concept. Answers to the questions posed at the end of each chapter are contained in Appendix Two. In some cases, the answers summarize the text, but in other cases they expand on the text. Thus, reading both questions and answers is suggested. The following questions paraphrase those in the book and highlight reflections on productivity presented.

PART I - INDIVIDUAL PRODUCTIVITY

    1.   Is Lines of Code (LOC) a good measure of individual performance?

    2.   How do other knowledge-type professionals monitor performance?

    3.   What is the number one mistake made when writing performance reviews?

    4.   Is "burnout" real?

5.   Did programmer productivity improve during the 1970s? How much?

PART II - PROJECT PRODUCTIVITY

1.   Can detailed project phase management have a negative impact on productivity?

2.   Does an advanced project management technique exist?

3.   What techniques are available to estimate large projects?

4.   How can the value of test time be quantified?

PART III - MAINTENANCE PRODUCTIVITY

1.   Can objectives be developed which monitor the performance of the maintenance manager?

2.   Is developmental documentation intended for the same purpose as maintenance documentation?

PART IV - DIVISIONAL PRODUCTIVITY

1.   How many unusual abend conditions would you expect when installing a ten manyear project?

2.   Why are poor standards written?

3.   Should auditors have project responsibility?

4.   In the year 2000, how will managers be trained?

PART V - CORPORATE PRODUCTIVITY

1.   Is data base utopia?

2.   Is it more cost effective to run seventy five minis or two mainframes?

3.   When computer hardware is virtually free, what will be the concern?

4.   What are the future barriers to productivity?

It should be pointed out that the five basic management functions (planning, organizing, staffing, directing and controlling) are not all explicitly discussed, but rather implied throughout the book. For example, answering questions related to recruiting talented people or resolving interpersonal relationships, such as handling disgruntled employees, is not within the scope of the book. However, the principles implied in the productivity techniques should definitely minimize personnel injustices and motivate the staff. Also, the five management functions do not receive equal treatment. The boundaries of the book are limited by the vastness of the subject--management.

The books and articles contained in suggested reading for each chapter are not intended as a thorough review of the literature. Rather, they simply represent readings the author has found interesting and useful.

Over the years, emphasis has changed from batch to online and from online to data base and distributed systems. However, the principles and concepts presented still apply, because managing for productivity is managing projects and personnel.

The book is intended for DP professionals or other managers with DP responsibilities, primarily in the commercial application environment. Also, the book is designed for use in a graduate level management computer science course.

I would like to thank John Brink, Steve Priest, and Ron Smith for reviewing the material at various stages of development. Also, appreciation is due to Tanya King and Charlene Gill who spent many hours typing and retyping the text. And last, I would like to thank both John Collins and Dick Tavella for encouraging research into productivity subjects, promoting a positive attitude and establishing the proper environment.

James R. Johnson
May, 1980

Contents

PART IV DIVISIONAL PRODUCTIVITY

PART V CORPORATE PRODUCTIVITY

LIST OF FIGURES

PART I

INDIVIDUAL PRODUCTIVITY

PRODUCTIVITY SUGGESTION: "SHOOT THE PROGRAMMER"

A User

PART I - INDIVIDUAL PRODUCTIVITY

Two facets of individual productivity, management techniques and productivity aids are presented as separate chapters in this part. The first chapter is divided into three sections: lines of code (LOC) and program estimating; LOC and performance reviews; and management techniques to improve individual performance, such as job rotation (Burnout Theory), internal resumes, and quantifying promotions.

Productivity aids are the second facet of individual productivity, and they are the subject of Chapter Two. It deals with tools or aids which affect the speed and quality of an individual's work. The most popular aids, marketed by IBM, are called Programming Productivity Techniques (PPTs). Also, a subjective attempt to quantify the impact of productivity aids is presented. Your opinion may differ, but the discussion provides a starting point. After commenting on the value of PPTs, Chapter Two discusses four other tools which directly relate to productivity - structure diagrams, standard modules, application generators, and self-generating code.

CHAPTER ONE

MANAGEMENT TECHNIQUES FOR INDIVIDUAL PRODUCTIVITY

Sections 1.1 and 1.2 clarify how LOC data can be quantified and its relationship to individual performance.

Note that an important distinction exists between using LOC as an estimating versus a performance monitoring tool. Basically, opposing arguments exist. Logic on one side states that knowledge must be quantified or it is of no value. As William Thompson stated in <u>Lord Kelvin</u>,

> When you can measure what you are speaking about,
> and express it in numbers, you know something about
> it; but when you cannot measure it, when you cannot
> express it in numbers, your knowledge is of meager
> and unsatisfactory kind; it may be the beginning of
> knowledge, but you have scarcely, in your thoughts,
> advanced to the stage of science.

Conversely, regarding individual performance, it has been said,

> If LOC is the measure of performance, every programmer
> knows, in his own black little heart, he can generate LOC.

Thus, using LOC to directly measure performance is not proposed. However, it is relevant as an estimating tool and as an input for individual performance reviews.

Section Three of this chapter explains important management practices which directly relate to improving individual performance: job rotation (burnout theory), internal resumes, and quantifying promotions.

1.1 LINES OF CODE (LOC) FOR PROGRAM ESTIMATING *

As experienced managers acknowledge, productivity is a function of selecting qualified people, establishing an adequate working environment, motivating personnel, and providing the proper management direction. When a group of individuals achieves high productivity, a positive atmosphere exists. Even though productivity may not be measured, those associated with the project know productivity is high. Optimal productivity is a result of dedicated, involved individuals working on "their" system. The adage "Put your heart in your work" still applies in the computer age. Management's responsibility is to provide individuals with this opportunity. Thus, it is concluded that managing is only a motivating process, not a productivity measuring activity, right?

Wrong. In this scientific world, productivity is productivity only if it is measurable. Knowing, feeling, or believing productivity is high is not, or soon will not be, acceptable in a programming environment. Faith is no longer an attribute of higher management. Proof of performance is a central issue. As maintenance and overhead increase, justification of the growing data processing budget becomes more difficult. First and second level managers are comfortable with existing management techniques, but higher level management is making the message clear: show us your productivity increases.

Granted, there is logic behind this philosophy; after all, the programming profession is still relatively unscientific. Yet the "success" of a software project today remains a subjective issue, since the performance of a programming project involves evaluating a composite of subjective factors the "quality" of people, the exactness of the requirement definition, the complexity of the hardware, the degree of innovation, etc. Quantitative measures do not exist for these factors. In the future, it may be possible to standardize functions (generalized requirements) so that meaningful comparisons can be made among software products, but progress in this area has not thus far been significant.

LOC by Default

There does exist one piece of information integral to all programming projects. It is not subjective, it is measurable, and by default it is the best data available. The measure is "lines of code." Opinions on the value of lines of code (LOC, for convenience) as an estimating standard are divergent. Some groups are ignoring LOC while others are utilizing self-developed standards.

Definitions are the Keys

References to LOC rates can be found, but the range of reported productivities varies from less than one LOC/hour to thirty or more. Is it possible that one group of individuals can outperform another by a factor of more than thirty? Why is there such a variation? More precise definitions of programs, mandays, and LOC clarify the situation.

A. Systems Programming Product

There are programs and there are programs. Depending on the definition of program, the cost of one may be nine times the cost of another. As Fred Brooks explains in <u>Mythical Man-Month</u> (Addison-Wesley, 1975, Reading, Mass.), programs exist at four levels of

---

*Adapted from Johnson, <u>A Working Measure of Productivity</u>, pp. 106 - 111.

complexity:

Level	Type of Program	Cost Factor
1.	program	1X
2.	programming product	3X
3.	programming system	3X
4.	programming system product	9X

According to his definitions, a "program" is run only by its author for a specific purpose. A "programming product" is differentiated from a program in two ways: (1) it is generalized, and (2) it is documented. Going from Level 1 to Level 2 increases the cost by a factor of three.

A "programming system" is a component which must be integrated, along with other components, into a system. Having to resolve interfaces increases the development cost over the cost to develop a "program" by an additional factor of three.

In the commercial data processing environment, the fourth level of complexity is the normal product. It has the attributes of both a programming system and a programming product. A programming system product requires nine times more resources than a "program" of similar size. The system is generalized, documented, integrated, and independent of its writers.

Implied in the term "cost" is a programming rate of production based on LOC. In other words, if nine LOC per hour were generated writing "programs" (the first level), then a productivity for a programming system product of one per hour would be expected.

When discussing rates of production, it is essential to define the level of complexity involved.

B. Mandays (Also see Appendix 1)

There are two clarifications required when quoting mandays. The first involves productive and nonproductive time. Generally, individuals are considered available for productive time somewhere between 50 percent and 80 percent of the total time. Vacations, illness, training, meetings, breaks, etc. account for the loss in productive time. Five mandays of productive time could equal ten total mandays based on that lower productivity factor of 50 percent. Thus, LOC rates may vary by a factor of two based on this observation.

Another item requiring clarification is related to project phases: definition, design, programming, testing, and conversion. Programming and testing generally comprise one-half of the total project. It is important to identify the phases included when addressing productivity rates. Is definition and design time included, or just programming and testing time? If LOC rates are computed using programming time only, the result is two times higher than it would be if time from all phases of the project were included.

Thus, manday definitions may account for a total variance factor of four: a difference of two based on productive/nonproductive time, and a difference of two based on program design time. In the extreme, three LOC per hour could equal twelve per hour based on manday definitions.

C. LOC

What then is an LOC? The simplest definition for an LOC is as follows:

> An LOC is a source of statement. It corresponds
> to any line on a coding sheet including internal
> comments and job control statements. It is installed,
> operational, and debugged to an acceptable level.

This all-inclusive definition facilitates collecting LOC data, since most installations utilize automated librarian systems to store and modify programs. Note that it does not include external documentation production.

There exist other, less general definitions which are worth discussing. In a COBOL program, for example, the following statements are LOC candidates:

> Procedure division (approximating number of verbs)
> Other divisions
> Comments
> Compiler control statements

The COBOL compile-listing outputs the following statistics:

1.	Number of total source records	1,733
2.	Number of data division statements	936
3.	Number of procedure division statements	525

The last output equates to the count of COBOL verbs, possibly the most revealing statistic about the complexity of a program. It is a much more refined measure of a program's complexity than the total number of source records. The ratio of verbs to total records is approximately 3.3 to 1 in this example.

Inconsistent definitions can account for dramatic differences in LOC rates. In a worst-case situation, definitions could account for a factor of 120! The assumptions have a multiplicative effect when the extremes are used; i.e.,

	Factor
Program definition	9
Mandays	2
Productivity factor	2
LOC (source vs. verbs)	3.3
Result (9x2x2x3.3)	120

As the example in Figure 1.1 shows, identical "productivities" could be reported as 0.375 LOC/hour or 45.0 LOC/hour. As usual, a meaningful comparison is only possible when assumptions are stated.

It is almost impossible to obtain comparative data on LOC, since very few quoted figures include mention of the assumptions. Historically, LOC data was not considered relevant in programming projects. Thus, it is not surprising to obtain incomplete information when searching for LOC rates.

The variation among programming rates is closely related to the definition of an LOC. For project estimating at a macro level (see Chapter Five), using the total number of source records is recommended, since it facilitates collecting and comparing programming rates among corporations. For micro or program estimating, Procedure Division verbs are recommended.

In the past, LOC has not proved to be a useful measure of program development productivity, largely due to definitional problems. For example, in Figure 1.1, two projects might report LOC rates differing by a factor of 120 due to differences in definitions.

	Project A	Project B
Program	--	yes
Programming Systems Product	yes	--
Design Time	500	55.5
Programming Time	500	55.5
Total Statements	10,000	10,000
Verbs	3,000	3,000
Productive Time Factor	1.0	0.5

$$LOC_A = \frac{\text{Number of verbs for programming system product}}{\text{Total man-days X productivity factor}}$$

$$= \frac{3000}{1000 \text{ X } 1.0} = 3.0 \text{ Lines/Day} = 0.375 \text{ LOC/hour}$$

$$LOC_B = \frac{\text{Number of statements for program}}{\text{Program time X man-days X productivity factor}}$$

$$= \frac{10,000}{55.5 \text{ X } 0.5} = 360 \text{ Lines/Day} - 45 \text{ LOC/hour}$$

$$\frac{LOC_B}{LOC_A} = \frac{45}{0.375} = \text{a factor of 120.}$$

Figure 1.1 Problems of LOC Productivity Reporting

How to Use LOC for Program Estimating

An example will be used to illustrate the use of LOC for program estimating. Consider Figure 1.2.

Assume a 500 LOC (procedure division verbs) program of medium complexity is to be written. The structure diagram, coding, compiling, and unit testing, requires 120 hours (24 hours/100 verbs x 500 LOC) based on the guidelines. The estimate of verbs and program complexity can be derived from any or all of the following: 1) individual judgment, 2) analogy with similar programs, and 3) identifying functions and summing the functions.

LOC estimating either implies knowledge of program function, or uses program function directly. The two articles commented on below expand on the "functional" estimating technique.

In "Project Planning and Control" (Donelson, Datamation, June 1976), module class or functional component is used as the basis for program estimating. The technique has similarities to the method proposed in this chapter. The function approach is taken one step further in "Taking the Measure of Programmer Productivity" (Crossman, Datamation, May 1979). This technique asumes that the time to develop a function within a program is independent of the LOC required; i.e., five to fifty LOC. The reader will have to judge the validity of this statement and the applicability of emphasizing function indirectly or directly in program estimating techniques. Independent of estimating, one significant advantage of concentrating on functions is that it facilitates standard modules in program development (see 2.2).

1.2 LOC AND PERFORMANCE REVIEWS

As stated in the introduction to this chapter, LOC is recommended as an indirect measure of performance versus a direct measure. This section discusses a variety of issues relating to performance reviews: a generalized system and other disciplines, requirements for a successful performance review program, and an example. Assessing individual performance equitably improves productivity and morale by acknowledging and rewarding people for their contributions.

A Generalized System and Other Disciplines

Attempting to establish a generalized individual performance monitoring system for programming personnel is a difficult task. However, by applying old fashioned management principles, it is possible to equitably assess individual performance.

DP is often compared with the discipline of engineering, which over the centuries has evolved to the level of a "science." How then does a disciplined science measure individual performance? Is a generalized technique available in the mature sciences? The answer to the second question is no. In response to the first question, there are as many techniques as there are companies--some are good and some are not so good.

The point is, for the vast majority of knowledge workers (professors, engineers, doctors, police chiefs, managers, etc.), no one has devised a general performance monitoring device in any industry or discipline. The reason is change. How many times does a knowledge worker repeat the same job under the same circumstances?

Program	Hours/100 Verbs			
Complexity	Step 1	Step 2-3	Step 4	Total
Easy	2	12	4	18
Medium	4	12	8	24
Difficult	8	12	12	32

NOTES:

A. Step Explanation

1. Structure Diagram--Graphically displays the logic and relationships in the program. Significant aid to program development. Level of detail is dependent on the situation.

2. Program Coding--Writing instructions on coding pad or on CRTs.

3. Compile--Eliminating compiler diagnostic errors.

4. Unit Test--Testing all logic paths in the program with generated or production data.

B. Program Complexity is a function of the following:

a. Number I/O files

1. Sequential processing vs. random
2. Number of record types

b. Complexity of function

1. Restructuring data
2. Condition checking
3. Data retrieval
4. Calculations

Subjectively, comparing a program relative to other programs is an appropriate way of classifying complexity.

Figure 1.2 Program Estimating Guidelines

Change is rampant in the programming profession. The 1970s brought programming productivity techniques (PPTs) plus online timesharing programming tools. Thus, since the objective of quantifying individual productivity has not been accomplished in similar disciplines which have experienced even less change, generalized individual productivity measurements prove impractical within the analysis/programming environment. But, within a profession, within an organization, performance monitoring is possible and desirable.

Requirements

Two basic requirements are necessary: 1) an incentive pay system; 2) competent first level management. If the environment does not support a merit pay raise philosophy, the whole subject becomes academic. Also, the individual writing the review must have knowledge about the tasks assigned and understand their difficulty.

Formal appraisals should be conducted once a year; however, informal discussions should be planned at midyear (see 1.3, Resumes, Internal). Assuming annual ratings and subsequent salary increases are based on relative rankings, a formal quarterly or semiannual review serves no useful purpose. Praise is appropriate anytime, but formal reviews and ratings should be kept on a yearly basis.

Should all appraisals be conducted during one period of time, say one month? Definitely yes. This is the only fair way to administer reviews. An anniversary date system does not facilitate consistent relative comparisons. Spreading the workload over the entire year is a poor excuse for less quality in reviews.

Example

The following paragraphs illustrate how to monitor individual performance.

Manager Joe has a group of ten working in various projects: three Senior Analysts, four Senior Programmers, three Programmers. For simplicity, assume the incentive system allows 35 percent of the personnel an above average rating. Joe's first job is to document what each individual accomplished during the year. To illustrate, an excerpt from the Programmer X's review written by Joe appears on the following page under ASSIGNMENT (see Figure 1.3).

The next step relates to Programmer X's contribution, skills, attitude, and effort to the previously defined specific assignments. Please note section titled CONTRIBUTION.

Step three, the manager ranks the individuals in each job classification (Senior Analyst, Senior Programmer, etc.) relatively, based on performance. Performance is, of course, based on previously defined objectives which are usually represented by task assignments and Gantt Charts. But with a relative system, an individual may complete all assigned tasks and not receive an above-average rating, because the competition did even better.

Finally, ratings are distributed for each classification. After all, more is expected from the senior individuals, right?

Performance monitoring is straightforward, but it is also subjective. The problem of change is solved by relative comparisons during each period of time. The most common management mistake in writing reviews is to start by documenting an individual's traits or talents versus starting by defining accomplishments. LOC, as the example illustrates, is an indirect input to performance. Incidentally, Programmer X received the Very Good rating among the three programmers.

ANNUAL PERFORMANCE REVIEW

Name	Position Title
Mr. X	Programmer

Division Department	Date Entered This Position
DP Systems Development	198X

1.   ASSIGNMENT

For the first six months, Mr. X worked on the XYZ project. This project was medium sized (3 manyears and 30,000 LOC). Mr. X participated in the implementation phase. His major responsibilities were: program and unit test the WXY subsystem (4,000 LOC), develop an integrated test plan, and participate in the systems test and installation.

For the last six months, Mr. X was assigned to the feasibility study phase of a large project. In this capacity, he conducted 15 interviews with user personnel and subsequently analyzed the data.

2.   Performance Rating:

☐UNSATISFACTORY ☐FAIR ☐GOOD ☐VERY GOOD ☐OUTSTANDING

3.   CONTRIBUTION

Mr. X's performance varied, depending on his specific tasks. His knowledge of structured programming and structure diagrams enabled him to be especially productive in the programming tasks. Mr. X equalled or exceeded the estimated program guidelines for all programs. His subsystem produced fewer errors than others of comparable size. During system test planning, Mr. X inadvertently excluded testing of one critical function. However, his extra effort demonstrated in system testing and implementation was one of the main reasons the system was successful.

On the large feasibility study, where strong conceptual skills and prior experience are helpful, Mr. X was not particularly effective.

```
SIGNATURES

EMPLOYEE  _____

MANAGER   _____

DATE      _____
```

Figure 1.3 Annual Performance Review

1.3 MANAGEMENT PRODUCTIVITY TECHNIQUES

The Burnout Theory endorses a management philosophy of job rotation/enrichment. In Part III, the theory is the basis for one of the management objectives for monitoring productivity of the maintenance manager. To aid the execution of planned job rotation, an internal job resume form is included. The form provides individuals with an opportunity to state their preferences and skills. The internal resume, as a secondary objective, provides a central document for obtaining past work accomplishments and experience. This information is input to help quantify promotional decisions, the final topic addressed in this section.

Burnout Theory*

The Burnout Theory is as follows:

> After two years on a system, a person reaches a productivity peak: he experiences "burnout." The only way to improve productivity further, assuming a promotion is not available, is a lateral move to a different system.

Why is this theory important? The Burnout Theory attacks boredom, fights complacency, dispels data processing mysticism, and more importantly, increases department productivity by developing more experienced data processing professionals. For example, take a person who has worked six years on an Accounts Payable System. No doubt the person feels very comfortable. But how receptive is that person to new concepts? Can the person freely explain the intricacies of the system to fellow workers? Has that person become complacent?

"Mysticism" is a term used here to explain a data processing system which is believed to be extremely complex. The tools of mysticism are undefined terms and outdated documentation. These tools are used to imply that the processing logic of a system is much more complex than it really is. A system is mystical when only one individual in an organization has the experience required to maintain it. The Burnout Theory proposes that mysticism can be dispelled by a planned rotation of responsibilities.

The theory promotes productivity by providing a constant challenge to an individual and by providing him a broader base of experience. Consider the careers of Ms. Burnout and Ms. Productivity as outlined below:

<u>Ms. Burnout</u>	
Program Training	1 year
Develop & Maintain Manufacturing System	<u>6 years</u>
	7 years

<u>Ms. Productivity</u>	
Program Training	1 year
Maintain Cost Accounting System	2 years
Maintain Personnel System	2 years
Develop & Maintain Marketing System	<u>2 years</u>
	7 years

---

*Adapted from Johnson, <u>Burnout</u>, p. 167.

Now, the question is: Who would be the best candidate to redesign a new Manufacturing System? The theory emphatically states that Ms. Productivity is the one.

The theory can only be implemented by positive management action. In other words, if you ask a person if he or she would like to make a lateral move, nine out of ten times the response will be negative. Reasons given will vary:

> The other system has too many problems.
> No one else knows my system.
> I don't know anything about Accounts Payable.
> I know my system users.
> I don't want to change.

It is not easy to insist on rotating people after two or more years on a system. Users will complain, and efficiency will decrease for one to three months. Implementing the Burnout Theory requires a conviction on management's part, and a belief that the benefits to individuals far outweigh short-term disadvantages.

Resumes, Internal

How does management choose the member of the organization who is best qualified to receive a reassignment that becomes available? How does one decide who has the talents, experience, and interest for the position?

The first response to the problem might be to collect information from various sources on potential candidates. Sources might include personnel file, manager's file, performance reviews, and training files. A more effective strategy is to maintain internal resumes on all individuals. These resumes would include information on interests and skills, catalogued under the following topics:

    I.   Personal
    II. Education
    III. Previous Employment
    IV. Other Interests
    V.   Company Experience
    VI. Work Preferences
    VII. Technical Skills

Maintaining internal resumes is recommended because the resume:

    1. Facilitates collecting appropriate data for decisions on promotions and re-assignments.

    2. Allows individuals to state their interests, skills, and preferences.

    3. Provides a basis for manager's midyear conversation with individual.

    4. Serves as a history of personal accomplishments.

Questions in the latter two sections are unique to Systems Development and Programming personnel within the Data Processing division. These sections provide individuals with a rare opportunity, and may contain surprises for the manager. For example, an individual may be interested in project management but have no interest in planning or administration, or an individual may prefer to work alone on programming tasks rather than interface with users. In each case, the answers set the stage for a valuable discourse.

The resume initially requires less than thirty minutes to complete, and yearly updates are recommended. A completed resume follows (see Figure 1.4).

Completed Individual Resume

The information on this form will aid management on the decisions relating to re-assignments. Also, it serves as a history of personal accomplishments.

I.   Personal:

Name: Karen Dunford
Married (Spouse's Name) : Joe
Children: Billy, Kay

II.   Education:

Mo/Yr

From To	Degree/Major	College	Honors
Sept 70 May 74	BS-Computer Sci	U. of Mo.	1st Honor Roll

III.   Prior company DP experience (including military):

Mo/Yr

From To	Company	System	Function
None			

IV.   Other job related accomplishments (teaching, publications, CDP, professional association, reserves, special awards or achievements):

Instructor for Speech Workshop 1976-77

Member of DPMA

Received CDP 1978

Figure 1.4 Completed Internal Resume

V. Company Experience

A. Dates and types of promotions:

    May 1974 - Started as Programmer

    Feb 1976 - Programmer/Analyst

    May 1979 - Senior Programmer/Analyst

B. List feasibility studies written, responsibility on projects, participation on implementations:

From	To	Functions/Major System	Accomplishments
6-74	8-76	Pre-Manufacturing	Implemented DD1 and DD2 Project (3-75 to 8-75), VBOT Efficiency Upgrade (1-76 to 3-76), System Control File Analyst (9-74 to 2-76)
9-76	1-78	Graphic Arts Tracking System	Participated in design, programming and installation of Phase I. Designed and installed file maintenance subsystem. Prepared detail design of Phase II.
2-78	Present	Marketing Information System	Wrote feasibility study for MIS and online account information. Responsible for system design programming and implementation of APS report. Also responsible for conversion and system test of MIS.

Figure 1.4 (Cont.)

	Interest Scale	Low				High
VI.	Work Preferences:					
A.	Type Work					
	1. CICS	1	2	3	4	(5)
	2. Data Base	1	2	(3)	4	5
	3. Mini	1	2	3	(4)	5
	4. Detail Design	1	2	3	4	(5)
	5. General Design	1	2	3	4	(5)
	6. Interfacing with Users	1	2	3	4	(5)
	7. Programming	1	2	3	4	(5)
	8. Working Alone	1	2	3	4	(5)
	9. Documentation	1	2	(3)	4	5
	10. Writing Reports	1	2	(3)	4	5
	11. Making Presentations	1	2	(3)	4	5
	12. Project Management	1	2	(3)	4	5
	13. Leading Other People	1	2	(3)	4	5
	14. Planning Schedules	1	2	(3)	4	5
	15. Administration	1	2	(3)	4	5
	16. Software Type Work	(1)	2	3	4	5
	17. Technical Advisor	(1)	2	3	4	5
	18. MARK IV Coord.	1	(2)	3	4	5
	19. Training Others	1	2	3	4	(5)
	20. Support	(1)	2	3	4	5
	21. Development	1	2	3	4	(5)
	22. Other (Specify)	1	2	3	4	5
	23.	1	2	3	4	5
	24.	1	2	3	4	5

Figure 1.4 (Cont.)

B.   Area

1. Engineering	1	2	3	4	5
2. Master Scheduling/TR	1	2	3	4	5
3. Forecasting/FGMS	1	2	3	4	5
4. Order Processing	1	2	3	4	5
5. Material Requirements Planning (MRP)	1	2	3	4	5
6. Manufacturing	1	2	3	4	5
7. Inventory Control/Dist.	1	2	3	4	5
8. Sales Reporting/Marketing	1	2	3	4	5
9. Accounting/Financial	1	2	3	4	5
10. Employee Information/ Payroll	1	2	3	4	5
11. Other: (Specify)	1	2	3	4	5

C. Comments on present responsibilities or future preferences:

Current assignment has been a challenge.
Would like to learn CICS and work with online system.

D. When would you like a re-assignment?

6 - 12 months, 1 - 2 years, future, not sure? 6 - 12 months.

E. Training Requested:

CICS

Figure 1.4 (Cont.)

VII. Technical Skills

1 = no experience
2 = some exposure
3 = working knowledge
4 = very knowledgeble
5 = expert

A. Languages

1. COBOL   1   2   3   4   (5)

2. Assembler   1   (2)   3   4   5

3. PL/1   1   2   (3)   4   5

4. MARK IV   1   2   3   (4)   5

5. FORTRAN   1   2   (3)   4   5

6. JCL   1   2   3   4   (5)

7. CICS   1   (2)   3   4   5

8. Other (TSO) 1   2   3   4   (5)

B. Design Techniques

1. HIPO   (1)   2   3   4   5

2. Warnier   1   2   3   4   (5)

3. Structured Pgmg. 1   2   3   4   (5)

4. Walk-throughs   1   2   (3)   4   5

5. Other   1   2   3   4   5

C. Project Phases

		Number Performed
Feasibility Study	Major = 1	Minor = 2
Design Phase	Major = 1	Minor = 3
User Training Step	Major = 1	Minor = 2
Conversion Step	Major = 1	Minor = 2
Implementation Step	Major = 1	Minor = 3

Figure 1.4 (Cont.)

Promotions - Quantifying That Subjective Feeling

Why are some promotional decisions so straightforward and others so difficult? It all depends on the performance differential of those under consideration for promotion: when one individual leads the pack, no problem. The concern arises when the group's performance is about equal. In this situation, the proposed technique can help quantify subjective feelings.

Deciding on the criteria for promotion is the first requirement. For example, the criteria for a first level management position might be the following:

1. Communication - oral and written ability.

2. Design expertise - knowledge of structural design methods, structured programming, different systems, CICS, or ability to adapt.

3. Attitude, image, maturity - respect in organization by peers.

4. Contribution - has earned promotion based on contribution.

5. Potential management skills - ability to plan, organize, and direct.

Next, gather data on each candidate. Internally generated resumes and prior performance reviews are the best sources. Based on this information, relatively rank the candidates for each criterion and assign points based on the ranking. If there are five candidates, the one with the greatest skill in communications receives one point; the next highest, two points, etc. Last, total the points by individual for all criteria. The individual with the lowest point total is your answer. The following example illustrates the procedure. Note that Mr. X is the best candidate for the position.

Candidates	Criteria 1	2	3	4	5	Totals
V	3	2	5	4	4	18
W	1	3	4	3	1	12
X	2	1	1	2	2	8*
Y	4	5	2	1	5	17
Z	5	4	3	5	3	20

One valuable refinement to this technique is group participation with other managers. After each person executes the procedure independently, the rankings are discussed one criterion at a time. Justifying rankings produces a healthy climate for revealing the candidates' strengths and weaknesses.

PART I

CHAPTER ONE DISCUSSION QUESTIONS

SECTION

1.1

1. Why do LOC statistics vary?

2. Is LOC a good measure of programming performance? Explain.

3. How can LOC be used to improve project productivity (Chapter 5)?

4. Is it possible to interweave discussions about individual productivity and project productivity (Chapter 5)? Why?

1.2

5. How do other knowledge-type professions monitor individual performance?

6. Should performance ratings have an impact on pay raises? Why?

7. Should individual ratings be relative to others in the same position, or based on an absolute scale? Why?

8. Should performance reviews emphasize an individual's general traits or talents? Why?

9. Can formal performance reviews be given too frequently? Explain.

1.3

10. Is burnout always present after an individual spends two years on a system? Explain.

11. Why are managers reluctant to rotate individuals to new assignments?

12. Why are internal resumes important?

13. After quantifying a promotional decision, you feel the top candidate is not the one for the job. What went wrong?

SUGGESTED READING

Brooks, Frederick P., Jr., The Mythical Man-Month Essays on Software Engineering, Addison-Wesley Publishing Company, Inc., 1975.

Couger, J. Daniel and Zawacki, Robert A., "What Motivates D.P. Professionals?", Datamation, September 1978, pp. 114-123.

Hall, Carl. L., "Evaluating Prospective Employees," Datamation, August 1975, pp. 32-36.

McCracken, Daniel D., "The Changing Face of Applications Programming," Datamation, November 15, 1978, pp. 25-30.

BIBLIOGRAPHY

Brooks, Frederick P., Jr., The Mythical Man-Month Essays on Software Engineering, Addison-Wesley Publishing Company, Inc., 1975.

Crossman, Trevor D., "Taking the Measure of Programmer Productivity," Datamation, May 1979, pp. 144-147.

Donelson, William S., "Project Planning and Control," Datamation, June 1976, pp. 73-80.

Johnson, J. R., "The Burnout Theory," Datamation, November 1974, p. 167.

Johnson, J. R., "A Working Measure of Productivity," Datamation, February 1977, pp. 106-111.

CHAPTER TWO

PRODUCTIVITY AIDS

Figure 2.1 reflects a subjective judgment of how various productivity aids have improved the LOC output of programming personnel. The LOC rates are based on a medium-sized project (three to eight manyears), and are calculated on total LOC (all source statements) and implementation mandays.

Modular programming (line 1), which was popular in the late 1960s and early 1970s, means segmenting a program into functional units. All units link to a root program. Complex programs are thus simplified from both a programming and maintenance aspect.

In section one, the highly publicized and best known Programming Productivity Techniques (PPTs) are discussed (lines 2-7). The next section covers structure diagrams (line 8), standard modules (line 11), application generators (line 12), and self-generating code (line 13). Report generators (line 9) are addressed in Chapter Eight under the topic Language Selection; and online compile and debug (line 10), in Chapter Six.

The major problem when comparing productivity gains expressed as LOC rates (once definitional aspects are resolved) is that no two projects have a common base of reference. Consider the differences possible in the following areas:

> Project Management Sophistication
> Training Program for New People
> Test Time Availability
> Detail of Specifications

Deficiencies in any of these areas would dramatically affect studies on productivity. For example, if project management typically did not review team members' work, and then structured diagrams were implemented (line 8) requiring project management review, the productivity improvement would easily exceed the estimated 5 percent.

Proving the relationship of LOC to productivity aids is impossible. The percent improvement is the author's opinion, and is no doubt debatable; however, the chart provides perspective, and can be substantiated at a macro level. Section 3 documents two major projects completed in 1979. The validity of the data is high, since detail testing statistics were requested from the project manager, and automated techniques were available. The project teams used the majority of production techniques discussed. The result was total LOC/manday of 48.7 and 48.5 for the implementation phases. It is incidental that the LOC/manday on these projects are almost identical. However, both projects do fall in the range ($\pm$ five LOC/manday) of what the graph predicts for the productivity techniques used.

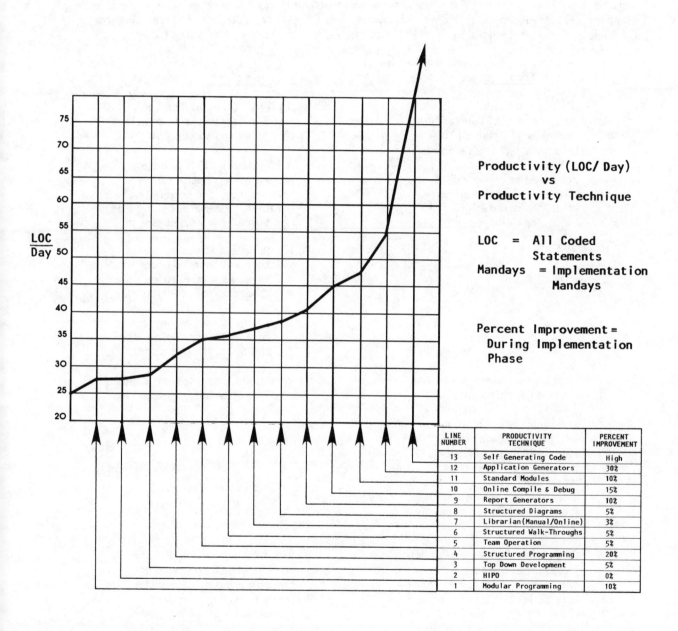

LINE NUMBER	PRODUCTIVITY TECHNIQUE	PERCENT IMPROVEMENT
13	Self Generating Code	High
12	Application Generators	30%
11	Standard Modules	10%
10	Online Compile & Debug	15%
9	Report Generators	10%
8	Structured Diagrams	5%
7	Librarian (Manual/Online)	3%
6	Structured Walk-Throughs	5%
5	Team Operation	5%
4	Structured Programming	20%
3	Top Down Development	5%
2	HIPO	0%
1	Modular Programming	10%

Figure 2.1 LOC and Productivity Aids

2.1 IBM's PPTs (Programming Productivity Technologies)

This section comments on IBM's six programmer productivity techniques which are line numbers 2-7 on Figure 2.1. Modular programming (line 1) was discussed in the chapter introduction. After explaining each IBM technique, the author's remarks are listed.

Line	Technique	Comment
2.	HIPO documentation is a design and documentation technique. Using HIPO throughout the development process, documentation is produced as a byproduct, eliminating the need for later documentation.	Of limited value. The technique becomes the end rather than a means to the end. A high level HIPO is nothing more than an outline in boxes across the page. The input-process-output diagram is a burden for two reasons: 1. It does not represent the sequence of program flow, as a structured diagram (ref. section 2.2). 2. There is no easy means to facilitate explaining why the processing is done.
3.	Top-Down Development imposes an architectural discipline on the sequence in which code modules are written, following previously identified functions. It reduces integration testing difficulties and promotes more orderly system development.	Very good, provides structure and organization to project.
4.	Structured Programming does for programs what sentences, paragraphs, pages, and chapters do for books: it makes them easier to read and understand. It also facilitates modification by other programmers.	Outstanding for its direct benefits. But structured programming also sets the stage for using standard modules, by allowing common functions to be identified. Structured programming requires practice, and it is possible to write a poorly structured program after a basic training class.

Line	Technique	Comment
5.	Team Operations is a concept which assigns a team to each project. The team usually consists of a chief programmer, a backup programmer, a librarian, and additional programmers and analysts as needed. This permits better definition and assignment of responsibilities, facilitating job interchanges.	The idea is obviously worthwhile, but how many chief programmers exist in an organization? By definition the chief programmer is 100 percent qualified. If organizations had such individuals no one would be worrying about productivity anyway. Thus, by all means, the team approach is recommended, but without qualified people, it will not guarantee success.
6.	Structured walk-throughs are conferences or reviews conducted by groups with the same objectives, but excluding management personnel. They are intended to review design, detect logic errors, develop test strategies, and promote the interchange of knowledge and viewpoints.	Very good. Also, easy to misuse by overusing--can waste time if no problem exists. For example, if a programmer is writing his third validate module on a system, there is no need for a formal walk-through.
7.	A Development Support Library is controlled by a librarian who assumes the administrative and clerical tasks imposed on programmers and managers. It provides up-to-date information on programs and test data as they are developed, both in computer-readable and human-readable form.	Unnecessary for project development (see 8.1, Documentation). Ninety-five percent of the functions initially proposed for the librarian can now be performed by programming personnel via online automated software such as TSO or ROSCOE. Also, contrary to popular opinion, programmers do not program eight consecutive hours all the time; they take breaks, too. Thus a librarian is unnecessry overhead. Maintaining documentation for a department is a necessary function, but quite distinct from the team librarian concept.

Line	Technique	Comment
7. (cont.)		One rather presumptuous suggestion proposed for the librarian was to "accept scribbled source statements from programmers and code them." Don't you think this might be a justified case of pampering?

NOTE: Four out of six isn't bad--even IBM isn't perfect.

2.2 OTHER PRODUCTIVITY AIDS

The four topics in this section (lines 8, 11, 12, & 13) are organized by popularity of use, with structured diagrams the most popular followed by standard modules, application generators and self-generating code. Although the idea of self-generating code has been popular in science fiction movies (as illustrated by "Hal," the intelligent computer in the movie 2001), it is no more than theory at this time.

Structured Diagrams (Line 8)

A variety of structured techniques exists to aid programming and design tasks. Consider the following popular structured diagram techniques:

> HIPO
> Warnier
> Structured Design
> Jackson Method

The value of structured diagrams is dependent on what they are used for: programming, system design, or maintenance. For programming tasks these design tools, which are essentially an outline of program logic, reach their greatest potential during complex program design. Flexibility is provided, since they can be general or detailed depending on the circumstances. Structured diagrams are better than pseudocode because more standardization is provided. The techniques which inherently display the sequence of execution are superior to those that don't; for example, HIPO does not. Having an encompassing standard that applies to all programs is not recommended, but if the logic is complex, structured diagrams are an excellent tool. They should be disregarded after implementation in favor of well-documented programs (see 8.1 Documentation).

Turning now from programming to other applications of structured diagrams, it is important to remember that these graphic display techniques do not design systems-- people do. For years, successful systems have been implemented using common sense and the English language as a means of communicating. System design is creative hard work which requires compromise and good judgment. It is obvious that some have listened to overzealous salesmen and are hoping techniques will eliminate design difficulty.

Commenting on the use of graphics by project phase adds perspective to their benefits:

Project Phase	Graphics Benefit	Alternatives
Feasibility Study	No	English
Design (User)	Yes	English
Programming, Program Design	Yes, very much	Pseudo Code
Maintenance	No	Structured Programming

This does not imply that graphics are of limited value; they can be very helpful in program and user system design if applied as a tool. However, fascination with the technique can divert concentration from the job at hand.

Standard Modules (Line 11)

Within the programs of a system or group of systems, similar functions are performed by multiple individual program modules. Existing statistical packages illustrate the standard modules concept. Other common examples are: table maintenance and look-up, field editing, file match and update, error reporting and initialization, and EOJ. All organizations, to a degree, standardize some functions; however, the amount of standardization possible far exceeds what typically occurs.

One of the best illustrations of how to waste programming resources on a function is the three-way file match. How many programmers have had to rethink this same problem? Plus, since it is complex, extensive testing is always required.

The implementation of standard modules means that the technique is practiced until 75% of the code in a given program (on the average) is generated. The act of programming with standard modules becomes a selection process where the applicable routines are combined to form a program. The impact on productivity and morale are obvious.

Also, as a by-product of standard modules, consistency results. Maintenance is simplified when programs are written in a "standard" way.

Application Generator (Line 12)

An application generator is a computer system for developing computer systems. It is the epitome of a high level language, and an extension of the standard module concept. Instead of the programmer piecing together common routines, a language is provided to perform the function.

For example, a new report is desired. The selection criteria, sort sequence, summary levels, and fields required are input via CRT in English language commands. The software takes over and generates the report. A further advancement of this concept is "query by example." Using this approach, a user simply states an example of the data desired. The software then interprets the logic implied in the example and produces a report from the desired data base.

The functions of editing, updating, and performing calculations are also part of the application generator. IBM's version of this software is called Application Development Facility (ADF). Using such a system, two dialogues exist. First, in the system design phase, the technique of trial and error is possible. This method implies a simulation of the system which dramatically improves the user's understanding of the system, and thus provides a functional system. The second dialogue is between the Programmer/Analyst and the application generator. This concept of programming is significantly different than today. In essence, the language selects the common modules which perform the desired functions. Familiarity with the language capabilities is required, but detailed programming is eliminated. However, there are limitations when complex processing logic is involved (see 8.2 Language Selection).

Self-Generating Code (Line 13)

With the traditional programming philosophy, all instructions are written and the computer executes the program based on predefined decision criteria: when the answer is produced, the machine rests.

An "adaptive self-modifying" programming philosophy requires a win or lose type of response for each answer. Also, the computer coding is written such that it can modify itself. In other words, the decision criteria is changed based on a negative response, a type of simulation with feedback. The best illustration is a game situation. Take tic-tac-toe, for example. If coding consisted of a general game plan (vs. a winning plan) and logic for modifying itself based on negative responses, then a learning program would exist. By allowing the program to play itself or another computer program many times (say one million), the adaptive program should be as good as a traditionally programmed one.

Now, there are restraining factors. First, the adaptive program would require extensive memory during execution and a significant amount of permanent storage (for remembering winning and losing strategies). Second, programming personnel have little or no experience in designing this type of program, since business applications do not require self-generating programs. Both of these reasons are based on economic factors.

However, hardware costs are decreasing and soon will no longer be a limiting factor. As for the economic justification, the possibility of androids becoming a household item in the future may provide adequate justification. In addition to performing household chores, androids could relate on an intellectual level if properly programmed. The key to production is a visual and audio input service, massive associate random access memory, and self-modifying programs.

Discussing the programming aspect, the traditional programming philosophy will obviously be too time-consuming for developing learning programs. The "self-adaptive" philosophy may be the only practical method of solution. Take, for example, the problem of increasing the android's vocabulary: a routine which adds definition and association of new words is obviously conceivable.

What a challenge for programmers! Develop an intelligent program that learns. The competition among manufacturers will be fierce. How would you like to system test a product in your home?

2.3 Project History

This section documents programming statistics on two relatively large projects completed in 1979. The first project was titled the Marketing Information System (MIS). It was comprised of two separate functions. The first function, the basic system, involved the generation of a summarized master file that contained thirty months of sales-related business transactions numbering approximately 500,000 per month. The second function, the dealer volume system, generated highly flexible, user-maintained sales reports for three separate marketing organizations. These reports were generated at the account level, and summaries were generated at four sales organizational levels.

The next project was called the Product Data Base (PDB). It incorporated data from multiple related files into a common data base. Also, from the user point of view, file maintenance capabilities were significantly improved.

Figure 2.2 indicates which productivity techniques were used.

Productivity Technique	MIS	PDB
1. Modular Programming	Yes	Yes
2. HIPO	No	No
3. Top Down Development	Yes	Yes
4. Structured Programming	Yes	Yes
5. Team Operation	Yes	Yes
6. Structured Walk-throughs	Yes	Yes
7. Librarian (Online)	Yes	Yes
8. Structured Diagrams	Yes	Yes
9. Report Generators	No	No
10. Online Compile & Debug	No	Yes
11. Standard Modules	Some	Yes

Figure 2.2 Productivity Technique Used

Figure 2.3 documents the mandays and LOC data (only DP team mandays are used in the calculations for both projects). Based on the assumptions stated, the productivity as measured by total LOC and DP team members is as follows:

$$\text{MIS} \qquad \frac{49,680 \text{ LOC}}{1020 \text{ mandays}} = \frac{48.7 \text{ LOC}}{\text{manday}}$$

$$\text{PDB} \qquad \frac{70,444 \text{ LOC}}{1453 \text{ mandays}} = \frac{48.5 \text{ LOC}}{\text{manday}}$$

The fact that these numbers are so close is coincidence. A range of ± five LOC/manday could be expected for similar projects. In this case there were two offsetting factors: online compile and debug (line 10) were used during PDB and not during MIS; on the other hand, the PDB project had to contend with new data base technology which was not used on the MIS project.

This data supports the author's proposed percentage improvement for productivity techniques. There are many assumptions and definitions stated which make comparisons with other organizations possible but admittedly difficult. Hopefully, the material will provide "perspective" to productivity discussions.

	Mandays	
Phase	MIS	PDB
Feasibility	240	235
Design	570	467
Implementation	1,020	1,453
Total Mandays	1,830	2,155
Total Manyears	7.63	8.98
	Installed	LOC
LOC	MIS	PDB
Total Macro LOC	49,680	70,444
Verbs as LOC	18,500	20,493

Figure 2.3 Mandays and LOC for Two Projects

PART I

CHAPTER TWO DISCUSSION QUESTIONS

SECTION

2.1   1.   Do you agree with the comments on the value of PPTs?

2.2   2.   When defining the benefits of structured diagrams, a distinction is implied between system design and programming. Do you agree with the author's ideas?

        3.   Why are HIPO-type graphics not recommended?

2.3   4.   Do the LOC/day on your projects fall on the graph presented (25-60 LOC/day)? Should they?

SUGGESTED READING

Fagan, M.E., "Inspecting Software Design & Code", Datamation, October 1977, pp. 133-144.

Walston, C.E. and Felix, C.P., "A Method of Programming Measurement and Estimation", IBM Systems Journal, Volume 16, Number 1, 1977, pp. 54-73.

Dolotta, T. A., ET AL., Data Processing in 1980-1985, John Wiley & Sons, 1976.

PART II

PROJECT PRODUCTIVITY

"WHY ISN'T JOHNNY CODING?"

D.P. Manager

INTRODUCTION

The following four chapters are devoted to managing development projects:

    Chapter Three - Four Stages of Project Management

    Chapter Four - Advanced Project Control

    Chapter Five - L O C and Project Estimating

    Chapter Six - Program Testing

Chapter Three explains the behavioral or motivational forces which have influenced the approach to project management within organizations. Is your organization currently in stage four?

Major projects are not planned every day - a year or more may elapse between projects. And this time gap is why Chapter Four is so important. Even experienced managers forget and often overlook one of the basic planning or monitoring requirements. The steps defined have stood the test of time with no additions or deletions.

As stated in the first section of Chapter One, the "success" of a software project, today, remains a subjective issue, since the performance of a programming system project involves evaluating a composite of subjective factors: the "quality" of people, the exactness of the requirement definition, the complexity of the hardware, the degree of innovation, etc. However, there does exist one piece of information which is an integral part of all programming projects. It is not subjective, it is measurable, and by default it is the best data available. The measure is "lines of code." Opinions on the value of lines of code (L O C) as an estimating standard are divergent. Some groups are ignoring L O C while others are utilizing self-developed standards. In Chapter One, the definitional aspects of L O C were addressed. The purpose of Chapter Five is to illustrate the value of using L O C in project planning at a macro level.

Chapter Six discusses three test and debug productivity tools: individual test reports; online programming; software justification; and testing metrics. The first tool assures that programming personnel are cognizant of testing resources. Even though the focus is on hardware resources, improved test plans result because testing statistics are available. Obviously, productivity is enhanced by test data generations and online programming. But how can the impact be quantified, what is it worth? And last, large project testing metrics are presented for references; i.e., estimating purposes.

CHAPTER THREE

FOUR STAGES OF PROJECT MANAGEMENT

Is project management on the verge of becoming a passé topic, or is there one stage of evolution remaining? This chapter proposes a fourth stage which receives impetus from top corporate management. The theory of four stages is based on motivational factors impacting on DP management.

Historically, DP management would not be thought of as perceptive; however, the force of self-preservation has recently drawn this trait to the surface. During the late 1960s and early 1970s, the DP manager became very concerned in one statistic: the average life of a DP manager was projected as two years. Perceiving this fact, the new managers decided to find a management approach which reduced the risk of the position. They did so, and as a matter of fact, they reduced the risk of project management to almost zero. But after operating in this mode for a few years and acknowledging that salary is generally related to responsibility and risk, the more perceptive managers, especially those familiar with Warren McFarlan's work (Nolan and McFarlan, "Effective EDP Project Management," Managing the Data Resource Function), proposed a refined operating procedure - portfolio management. As Figure 3.1 illustrates, the stages are:

I.	Brute Force	Prior 1965
II.	Search for Performance	1965 - 1975
III.	Creeping Commitment	1975 - 1980
IV.	Portfolio	1980+

The characterisitics of each stage will be discussed in sequence.

BRUTE FORCE STAGE

Most, if not all, of the project due dates set prior to 1965 were missed. But this is understandable. The technology was new and management operated literally by the seat of its pants. However, after a due date slipped, the philosophy was to work as hard as physically possible (eighty-hour weeks) until the job was completed. Higher than average productivity (effectiveness of the project team) resulted from dedication and long hours. The status reports simply stated the system would be implemented when it was finished.

The potential of DP applications benefits plus an optimistic attitude by top management provided DP management with medium longevity - job security.

Also, most projects were not large (less than ten manyears), so budget overruns were not too significant.

SEARCH FOR PERFORMANCE STAGE

Missing project dates on small to medium-sized projects was not disastrous. But the first large project in a corporation got the attention of everyone. Cost overruns ranged from a few hundred thousand to millions. Control and monitoring steps were the logical outcome. Detail time reporting systems developed also, but these tools did not "bail out" projects. Top management was temporarily pacified, based on this action, since some action is preferable to none, but measurement itself did not improve the situation; heads began to roll, the fear of losing a job increased, the DP manager's perception resulted in Phase III - creeping commitment.

	CHARACTERISTIC	I Brute Force	II Search for Performance	III Creeping Commitment	IV Portfolio
1.	Time in Vogue	Prior 1965	1965-1975	1975-1980	1980+
2.	DP Mgt. Motivation	Optimism	Fear	Safety	Confidence
3.	Top Mgt. Acceptance	Fair	Poor	Fair	Good
4.	DP Mgt. Longevity	Medium	Low	Medium	High
5.	Number of Late Projects	Most	All	None	A Few
6.	Due Dates Established	Yes	Yes	Floating	Yes/No
7.	Mgt. Technique	Seat of Pants 80 Hours	Time Report- ing, Stand- ards	Specializa- ation, Audit- ing, Pert/ CPM	History, Analogy, Judgment
8.	Real Produc- tivity	Med-High	Med-Low	Low	High

Figure 3.1 Stages of Project Management

-37-

CREEPING COMMITMENT STAGE

At last, job security. Limiting the commitment of a project to one phase at a time assured that overruns would never exceed 20-25% for a phase. After all, the definition of a phase is never so precise that one could prove beyond reasonable doubt it is not completed. Thus management, exercising its own discretion, could complete a phase or define a new one prior to excessive overruns. As one might expect, the creeping commitment phase produced extensive (unnecessary) documentation and generally a low overall project productivity.

Ancillary tools were associated with this phase - productivity measures, audits, quality control, defect removal, etc. But the key was one-step-at-a-time. Risk is virtually eliminated if numerous steps are defined. Typically, a life cycle might contain twelve phases, as illustrated in Figure 3.2.

But the logic for gradual commitment was also the reason for advancing to the next stage. Top management realized that this was not management, but rather a "cop-out" - anyone (even the previous DP manager) could predict one to three months in the future. Also, the creeping commitment concept promoted indecision, and consequently wasted resources. Thus, the final stage of evolution was ready to emerge.

PORTFOLIO STAGE

In the fourth and final stage of project evolution, DP management is under pressure to combine project risk and also commitment on due dates. Combining the portfolio concept with a simpler version of project phases is the answer.

Warren McFarlan defined three variables which determine the management risk associated with projects: structure, technology, and size. He concluded that a large, unstructured (very innovative), high technology project is risky even if well managed. The portfolio concept groups projects of similar risk - somewhat analogous to a portfolio of financial securities. Top management has the responsibility for establishing the number of high risk projects. For example, it is not necessarily good to have all ultra-conservative projects or all risk projects. Once guidelines are established, DP management manages projects in one of two ways: due date commitments or research. The research projects are the high risk efforts, such as installing distributed system with new software and hardware. From the start, management understands the consequences of such a venture, and realizes that cost and time estimates may double. Thus, the budget is open-ended, and it is reviewed periodically for a "go, no-go" decision.

The nonresearch type projects, which ideally comprise the majority of work, are managed with greater authority. Combining several phases from the creeping commitment stage into one phase titled Feasibility Study brought respectability back to DP. Top management expected the feasibility study to provide adequate information for a "go, no-go" decision. Thus, those performing the study understood their charter - enough data should be gathered for the scope of the recommendation to be known with an acceptable degree of confidence. Using historic project data, analogy, and judgment, DP managers do a reasonably good job of project estimating.

A simpler version of project phase is shown in Figure 3.3. The main difference between the creeping commitment and portfolio stage is that the first six steps of the former are condensed to two phases in the latter. The feasibility and design phases have more measurable or meaningful milestones (objectives/output).

	Guideline Percentages		
	Degree of Firm's Commitment	Average Phase Expense	Cumulative Project Expense
Initial Investigation	0	0	0
Preliminary Systems Study	10	5	5
Systems Planning Study	25	10	15
Systems Requirements	50	10	25
Systems Specifications	60	5	30
Technical Requirements	70	5	30
Programming	85	30	65
Implementation Planning	85	5	70
User Training	85	5	75
Systems Test	90	5	80
Conversion	90	19	99
Post Implementation Reviews	95	1	100

Figure 3.2 Gradual Commitment

Phase	Percentage of Total Manpower	Objectives/Outputs/Tasks
Initial Investigation	0	Responsibility identified Formal request documented Estimate scope for feasibility study
PROJECT BEGINS		
1. Feasibility Study	5-15	Adequate data for management Decision - "GO" or "NO-GO" Analysis activity Variable depth Formal Study Rate of return calculated
2. Design	25-35	User design contact "complete" at end of phase Functional specifications Estimate of remaining phases
3. Implementation	50-70	Programming Education, System Test Turnover documentation Conversion
PROJECT ENDS		
Post Implementation Audit		Review of entire project.

Figure 3.3 A Simpler Version

The portfolio approach represents an optimal compromise for project managers and corporate executives. It produces a high level of project productivity. However, there is one factor which has the potential of cycling an organization's evolution backwards - overconfidence. Managing complex DP projects is, by its nature, a challenging task.

PART II

CHAPTER THREE DISCUSSION QUESTIONS

Can the creeping commitment stage of project management have a negative impact on productivity?

SUGGESTED READING

Gibson, Cyrus F. and Nolan, Richard L., "Managing the Four Stages of EDP Growth," Harvard Business Review, Number 74104, January - February 1974.

BIBLIOGRAPHY

Nolan, Richard L. and McFarlan, Warren F., "Effective EDP Project Management," Managing the Data Resource Function, West Publishing Co., 1974, pp. 293-307.

CHAPTER FOUR *

ADVANCED PROJECT CONTROL

Most discussions of project management expand on the major phases of a project: Feasibility Study, Design, Implementation (Programming, System Test, Acceptance Test, and Conversion). Within each phase, project management texts describe system tools such as interview questionnaires, input/output layout sheets, control procedures, etc. Most literature also contains advice or suggestions on what to do and what not to do; for example, requiring design signoff is a "what-to-do."

The scope of this project control procedure is limited to the basic concepts. Its content is independent of the project phase, and deals with the fundamentals of control. A sports analogy is a football play, where executing the basic functions (blocking and tackling) is independent of the particular play or game. Although a project control procedure is only one aspect of project management, it is an essential aspect.

The following procedure lists steps which can be used to plan and monitor a project or any phase of a project. The project control steps are divided into the following segments: planning and monitoring. It is assumed that the scope of the project has previously been defined. Figure 4.1 shows an illustration of how the ten step procedure relates to the basic working documents: work plan, PERT chart, and Gantt chart.

PLANNING A PROJECT

Step 1: Define Tasks. A written description of each task is required. This description provides a common reference point for defining responsibilities. When what has to be done is known, realistic schedules are possible. The ability to define tasks is directly dependent on the nature of the activity. If one-hundred COBOL-F programs have to be converted to COBOL VS, and five have been converted on a pilot basis requiring two mandays each, then the total effort of the project can be defined with a reasonable probability of accuracy.

Conversely, task definition has the highest probability of error at the completion of system design on a large innovative project. For example, assume a managment information system (MIS) is proposed for product managers of a large corporation. The MIS objective is to assimilate forecast, production, inventory, cost, and sales data into useful decision-making information. For a complex system such as this, it is humanly impossible to complete a realistic final design. The difficulty of identifying useful information prior to physically receiving reports and using the system in a working environment cannot be exaggerated.

System Design is not complete at the end of system design. Approval signatures are only an attempt to obtain a complete final design. They do not assure it. Don't attempt to do all phases of a project at once; add to the programming effort for unanticipated design changes. Be realistic, not optimistic. Defining the optimal system, which serves the user's needs is dependent on the ability of people to define in advance all their information needs. There is no technique available which will identify all required tasks in advance, so allow for the unknown. The technique of structured design provides a solution which is usually more flexible in its ability to accommodate the unknown and inevitable changes.

---

*Adapted from Johnson, <u>Advanced Project Management</u>, pp. 24-27.

Schematic of Project Control Steps And Working Documents

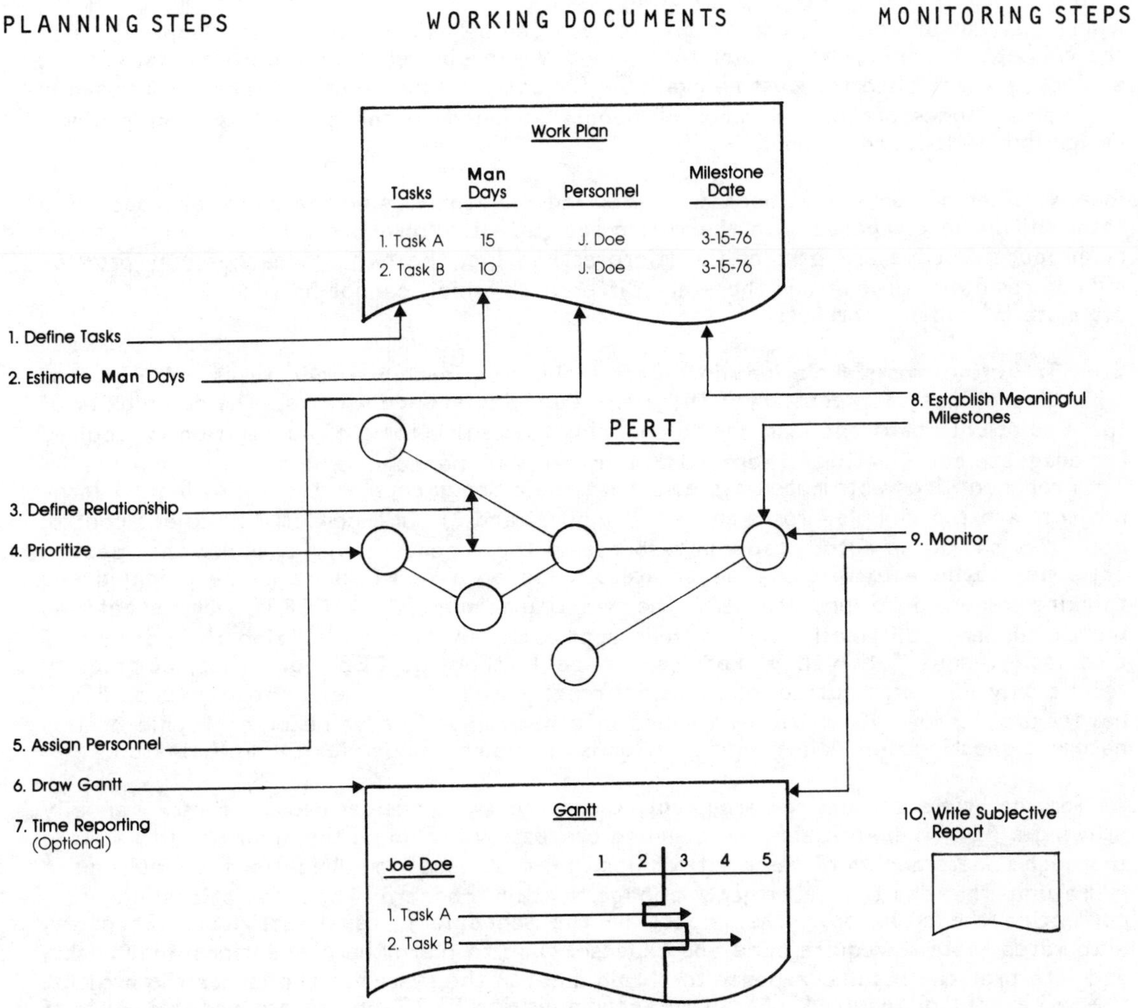

PLANNING STEPS   WORKING DOCUMENTS   MONITORING STEPS

Work Plan

Tasks	Man Days	Personnel	Milestone Date
1. Task A	15	J. Doe	3-15-76
2. Task B	10	J. Doe	3-15-76

1. Define Tasks

2. Estimate **Man** Days

PERT

3. Define Relationship

4. Prioritize

8. Establish Meaningful Milestones

9. Monitor

5. Assign Personnel

6. Draw Gantt

7. Time Reporting
(Optional)

Gantt

Joe Doe   1 2 3 4 5

1. Task A

2. Task B

10. Write Subjective Report

Figure 4.1 Project Control Schematic

Step 2: Estimate Mandays. The accuracy of the manday estimates is a function of the type of project. For small projects, or in the programming stage on large projects, mandays for specific tasks (ignoring design changes) can be estimated very accurately. However, when performing general system design, the completion of one task may result in the definition of additional tasks. It is a good idea to compensate by doubling the mandays for each task. Consider that people are actually available for productive work only half the time, and double initial estimates.

The micro approach in estimating involves rolling up a number of detail estimates to obtain the total effort. For programming tasks, the level of detail is at the module level, where analysis of lines of code by module type can be helpful. The macro approach uses the concept of analogy to predict total manday and elapsed time requirements. To use analogy, project histories must be available for comparisons. Some of the factors used in analogy are lines of code, number of people assigned to the project, size of project, design innovation, and technology.

Ideally, after mandays have been estimated independently using the micro approach, the total should be compared with the macro results. If allowances for unknown tasks and nonproductive time are part of the micro estimating, the two approaches may produce similar results. However, if there are differences which cannot be resolved, the larger estimate is probably correct.

Step 3: Define Tasks Relationship. Define the relationship among tasks. A PERT or CPM diagram may be necessary if there are multiple dependent tasks. The complexity of these relationships might lead one to conclude that some form of automation is required for adequate coordination. There exist many program packages which automate Steps 3 - 7. Proponents for automated systems base their arguments on the following: 1) large projects are too complex for manual techniques, and 2) time-consuming project control activities should be automated. In response to these contentions, consider the specific activities to be automated. The greatest value of a PERT chart is the planning and thinking required to prepare it. The maximum number of PERT chart events an individual can realistically work with is approximately fifty. Utilizing the concept of modularity, any of the fifty modules can be further sub-PERTed. Thus, complexity results only if a large number of boxes are represented on one page. Most texts on PERT have examples of 300 or more modules in a network. The value of a graphic of this nature is questionable. When segmentation is utilized, the complexity is eliminated.

As for the "time consuming" argument, there are two considerations. First, manually drawing a PERT network aids the planning process by providing the planners with a more thorough understanding of the relationships. In most cases, modifications do not require redrawing the chart. A project manager's main concern when deviations occur is correcting the situation. The impact on the schedule is usually obvious. Secondly, automated systems require time and expense: time to learn the conventions, input data, and interpret the results; expense to obtain and run the system. The larger the project, the more control required. Standard techniques for PERT charts are possible with or without an automated system.

Step 4: Prioritize Tasks. Since resources are finite, all tasks cannot be accomplished concurrently. Thus, priority tasks are those on the critical path or those which may be potential problem areas.

Step 5: Assign Personnel. When assigning personnel to tasks, consideration should be given to experience and talents of individuals. Manday estimates in Step 3 were made assuming an average experience level. If an inexperienced individual is on the project, manday estimates should be adjusted. Even for personnel with equivalent experience, productivity can vary substantially.

Time should be allowed for training new personnel on technical skills. Also, a one-month project orientation period is generally required. After tasks are assigned, total the mandays for each person. Compare this total to the available days. If an imbalance exists among individuals, tasks should be reassigned. This comparison may appear obvious, but it is frequently overlooked.

Step 6: Draw Gantt Charts. Gantt tasks in priority order, considering defined relationships among tasks. Since individuals usually work on multiple tasks, elapsed days are greater than task manday estimates. To assure that available mandays equal Gantted mandays, total the mandays Gantted for a month and compare the result with the available mandays.

Remember, one of the main factors impacting programming tasks is test turnaround time. Poor turnaround time can easily double the elapsed time estimates that were made assuming average turnaround.

Step 7: Automated Time Reporting. Tasks can be loaded into an automated time reporting sytem if one is available. Do not necessarily load the lowest level task since maintenance of the system can become burdensome. Also, the definition of lower level tasks may change as time progresses, especially in general system design.

The purpose of the automated system is to monitor time spent on tasks and provide a historic record of time spent on phases of the project. An automated system should not be used to schedule work.

Step 8: Establish Meaningful Milestones. A meaningful milestone is a point in time when a task or number of tasks can be completed 100 percent. The following are examples:

1.   Report package documentation sign-off
2.   Completion of the system test plan
3.   Phase I implementation

One important factor, which is often overlooked when milestones are defined, is an explanation of how and who will sign off on the milestone. For example, in number one above, assume that the group preparing the documentation also decides when it is completed. With this delegation of responsibility, regression to the 98 percent complete rule in order to stay on schedule is possible. When milestones are defined, specify how the tasks will be acknowledged complete, and who will sign off on the completion. An independent individual is the preferable selection.

Step 9: Monitor. There are two types of monitoring which are helpful - individual and project. Individual monitoring is best done by updating Gantt charts with a line showing current status versus expected status at a point in time. Monitoring actual manhours expended versus planned is also possible; however, it does not easily provide an overall visual status as Gantt charts do.

Project monitoring is based on the predefined meaningful milestones. It is very important to reconcile variations from each milestone. If the first milestone date is missed by a considerable margin, then there may be good reason to re-evaluate all the remaining projections. This step implies that the project manager: 1) understands the tasks, 2) knows why deviations from the plan occur, and 3) takes appropriate action to correct out-of-control situations.

Extensive project control procedures can have an adverse impact on productivity. Good project control is not elaborate control. When dates slip, there is a tendency to over-control and define detailed procedures. For example, instead of monitoring overall progress weekly or monthly, a procedure to monitor progress day-by-day may be implemented. Thus, individuals and the project manager would have to maintain considerable detail data in an attempt to report on a daily basis. Even more important than the extra time required for elaborate controls is the fact that they can divert the attention of a project manager from the relevant issue of finding the real problem.

Success is not dependent on reporting technique. Procedures should not be a burden on project managers, but rather an extension of their control techniques. Assuming the basic steps are followed, there are as many different variations as there are project managers.

Some individuals find it difficult to write concise reports, and others work effectively with rough Gantt charts and note cards. The point is, a control procedure should not force project managers to standardize all aspects of their jobs. Productivity is greatest when a project manager sticks with the fundamentals and is allowed to function in an individual, effective manner.

Step 10: Write Subjective Report. In addition to the objective measures above, a subjective report should be completed periodically by the individual responsible for the project. Numbers and charts do not describe the attitude or motivation of the project team. It has been said that individuals on a successful project always have a warm feeling about the progress. A subjective report represents a personal appraisal of the project status.

WHY PROJECTS ARE LATE

The major reason for project lateness involves task definition and manday assignments, and these factors account for 80 percent of the cases. Good project control techniques do not significantly change the amount of resources required to complete a phase. However, by allowing time for unknown tasks and by realistically allowing for nonproductive time, the source of estimating errors will be reduced. The remaining 20 percent of project lateness cases are caused by not executing a step successfully because of poorly defined milestones, a missing PERT chart, burdensome control procedures, or poor programming techniques. Recently the last item has received much attention. Structured programming will definitely help minimize this factor.

SUMMARY

The ten steps, seven for Planning and three for Monitoring, apply to any phase of a project. Obtaining project control is not easy. It requires hard work, involvement, good judgement, and an "advanced" procedure. "Advanced" is not synonymous with "sophisticated." Proper execution of the basic steps, with stress on the fundamentals, is the answer.

PART II

CHAPTER FOUR DISCUSSION QUESTIONS

1. The cost factor is implied in manday effort, but should it be stressed more in the procedure?

2. Does detailed monitoring necessarily increase productivity?

BIBLIOGRAPHY

Johnson, J. R., "Advanced Project Management," Journal of Systems Management, May 1977, pp. 24-27.

CHAPTER FIVE *

PROJECT ESTIMATING

TAKING THE MEASURE

In order to establish a data base for comparisons using LOC, a total of sixteen projects were audited. Project completion dates ranged from 1970 to ones completed in 1978 (see Figure 5.1).

Definitions are as follows:

1. All projects produced systems programming products.

2. Manday figures include both productive and nonproductive time. They were obtained on a macro level; i.e., by multiplying the number of people assigned to projects times the duration of assignment. The mandays include time spent on all phases of the project. Also, since users were assigned as analysts in many cases, their time on the project is part of the total. The manday totals may vary by + 15% due to historical inaccuracies. However, an average figure taken from this data should negate compensating errors and thus improve accuracy.

3. LOC was obtained from automatic librarian counts. Thus, comments and all other statements are counted as LOC. For older systems, adjustments were made for the code added since implementation.

Also, since common record layout definitions were used extensively in different projects, and since these common definitions are coded only once (even though called by many programs), they were counted one time only. Based on the techniques used to gather data, error rates for LOC could be as high as + 10 percent. The averaged result would be more accurate. Figure 5.1 lists the projects in descending order of mandays expended. The first observation is that a strong relationship exists when LOC/hours are compared for small and large projects (large projects are defined as two-plus manyears). On the average, small projects produced over three times more coding per hour than large projects (2.9 vs. 8.7). This would be expected, based on increasing numbers of both interfaces and communication links.

The LOC rates did reflect, in a general way, management's subjective opinion of the "productivity" of the various projects. Factors such as design difficulty (innovation), level of technology, and quality of staff are considered in the subjective opinion. On Project "B" (12.5 LOC/hour), all the factors which tend to impair progress were absent. The team was highly motivated and working with known technology. One of the large projects, Project "J", had one of the highest rates (5.1 LOC/hour). The project was an Employee Information System which included Payroll, Benefits, and Personnel subsystems. The extent of innovation was limited, as well as the amount of new technology involved. Thus, a high level of productivity could be anticipated.

---

*Adapted from Johnson, <u>Working Measure of Productivity</u>, pp. 106-111.

Project	Man-Days Total	Recorded Statistics for Commercial Projects Lines of Code ($\times$1000)			Lines/Man-Day	Lines/Hour
		Batch	On-Line	Total		
A	40	3.1	0.0	3.1	77.5	9.7
B	56	5.6	0.0	5.6	100.0	12.5
C	70	4.0	0.0	4.0	57.1	7.2
D	110	2.7	3.2	5.9	53.6	6.7
E	240	2.0	12.0	14.0	58.0	7.5
						Average 8.7
F	528	10.0	0.0	10.0	18.9	2.4
G	924	36.0	5.0	41.0	44.4	5.6
H	924	33.0	1.0	34.0	36.8	4.6
I	3432	60.0	0.0	60.0	17.5	2.2
J	3432	140.0	0.0	140.0	40.8	5.1
K	3960	46.0	29.0	75.0	18.9	2.4
L	4752	80.0	0.0	80.0	16.8	2.1
M	8712	190.0	0.0	190.0	21.8	2.7
N	10,560	133.0	7.0	140.0	13.6	1.7
O	14,784	130.0	0.0	130.0	8.8	1.1
P	79,200	784.0	126.0	910.0	11.5	1.4
						Average 2.9

Figure 5.1 Project Statistics

Project "O" had the lowest L O C rate. Since it was the first system of its type in the industry, a lower productivity resulted.

Concluding, L O C can be used at a gross level for project estimating. In other words, the fact that the average L O C rate for large projects is 2.9 is useful. If new technology and large-scale innovation are inherent in the project, the L O C rate will be lower.

The projects in the study were restricted to the commercial data processing environment. This implies a high level language and does not include developing operating systems and compilers. As Fred Brooks (The Mythical Man-Month Essays on Software Engineering, Addison-Wesley, 1975) stated:

> My guideline in the morass of estimating complexity
> is that compilers are three times as bad as normal
> batch application programs, and operating systems
> are three times as bad as compilers.

Using this concept, and converting the study rate for large projects (approximately three L O C/hour) to operating systems and compiler rates, produces consistent results (see Figure 5.2).

Results versus Brooks' Results

Product Complexity	This Study Hourly	Yearly	Brooks' Estimate
Batch Programs	3 LOC/hr.	6,336	6-9,000
Translators	1 LOC/hr.	2,112	2-3,000
Operating System	0.3 LOC/hr.	704	600-800

Figure 5.2 L O C Comparison

WHAT NEXT?

It is appropriate to discuss action items relating LOC to definitions and project estimating. The first task is to complete a data base of historical LOC information. Implementing a post audit procedure to capture the information immediately after a project is completed is suggested. The following data should be included (or their non-COBOL equivalents, see Chapter Eight - Post Implementation Audit for more specifics):

> Type of product (level: program, program product, etc.)
> Design time
> Programming language
> Programming time/type program (validate, update, report, etc.)
> Total statements/type program
> Data division statements/program
> Number verbs/type program
> Productive time factor

Having this data will allow meaningful comparisons among departments, divisions, and corporations.

After the data is collected, it can be used as a measure on a macro or project level. Based on this study and others, a relationship has been established between LOC rates and the size of a data processing system. Thus, if LOC are known, it is possible to estimate the mandays required for a project. It could be argued that knowing LOC implies knowing the scope of the project, and if the scope is known, mandays can be estimated directly. The only argument which established LOC as a legitimate estimating tool is experience with the technique. After initially challenging the concept, the author has found it useful, and is now a supporter of the technique.

LOC AS A TOOL FOR ESTIMATING

As discussed in Chapter Four (Step 2 - Estimating Mandays), there are two basic techniques for estimating project effort or duration:

A.   Macro - LOC and Analogy

B.   Micro - Work Plan and Task Definition

The techniques are not mutually exclusive and may both be used to estimate total project scope. First, the macro approach will be discussed. To utilize the LOC ranges stated above, two inputs are required: 1) an estimate of LOC, and 2) complexity of the project. A system flow chart (balloons and boxes), is a requirement of a feasibility study and is the basis for estimating the size of each program (LOC). Using program functions and analogy as an estimating base will produce reasonable results.

Predicting the complexity of the project is more subjective. The overriding parameter is project size but two other elements are important: project innovation and degree of technology (adapted from: Nolan, Richard L. and McFarlan, Warren F., "Effective EDP Project Management", Managing the Data Resource Function, West Publishing Co., 1974, pp. 293-307). Innovation refers to the design difficulty - is the function of proposed system completely new? How difficult will it be to define the system? For example, an employee information application may be rated as having low innovation. On the other hand, a state-of-the-art product information system would be rated as having high innovation. Unfamiliarity with new hardware or a new programming language is taken into account by the degree of technology. A high technology project might be the first mini-computer implementation. Figure 5.3 illustrates a comparison of two large projects which had similar LOC output. Obviously, a subjective interpretation is required. By using the data in this chapter as guidelines, macro manday estimates for projects can be projected. Take the following example:

Assume there are 35 programs totaling 60,000 LOC. Based on project organization, technology, and degree of design structure or innovation, a productivity rate is selected. Assume 3.5 LOC/Hr is judged reasonable, then:

$$\frac{60,000 \text{ LOC}}{3.5 \text{ LOC/Hr}} = 17,143 \text{ total hours or 2,143 mandays}$$

Assuming four individuals on the project:

$$\frac{2,143}{4} \text{ mandays} = 536 \text{ elapsed days}$$

or 27 elapsed manmonths
or 2.2 elapsed manyears

Now turning to the second estimating technique, the micro approach. A work plan is a list of all defined tasks and the associated manday estimates. By summing the mandays, the total manpower is computed. Usually a factor should be added for unknown tasks. For example:

Tasks 1-50 = 2,000 mandays

Plus 20% unknown = 2,400 mandays

Assuming four people assigned,

$$\frac{2,400}{4} = 600 \text{ elapsed days}$$
or 30 elapsed manmonths
or 2.5 elapsed manyears

Please see Appendix 1 for a definition of a manday as used throughout this book.

PARAMETERS		A/P	ED
1.	Technology Involved	HIGH	LOW
2.	Innovation of System	MEDIUM	LOW
3.	Maximum Number of People (DP)	9	13
4.	Expertise of Personnel	AVG-EARLY VERY GOOD-LATE	VERY GOOD
5.	Programming Elapsed Time	22 MONTHS	10 MONTHS
6.	Project Elapsed Time	34 MONTHS	22 MONTHS
7.	Number of Programs	100	20 NEW 90 EXISTING
8.	Lines of Code	46,000 BATCH 29,000 ONLINE	59,000 NEW 37,000 OLD
9.	User Involvement	HIGH	LOW
10.	System Interfaces	HIGH	MEDIUM
11.	System Test Elapse Time	5 MONTHS	3 MONTHS
12.	Test Time	VERY GOOD	EXCELLENT
13.	Total Cost (not including test time)	$390,720	$371,360

Figure 5.3 Project Analogy

PART II

CHAPTER 5 DISCUSSION QUESTIONS

1. Can any corporation use the guidelines stated in this chapter for estimating?

2. Why are small projects so much more productive?

3. Should LOC standards be used at the program level?

SUGGESTED READING

Walston, C. E. and Felix, C. P., "A Method of Programming Measurement and Estimation," IBM Systems Journal, Volume 16, Number 1, 1977, pp. 54-73.

BIBLIOGRAPHY

Brooks, Frederick P., Jr., The Mythical Man-Month Essays on Software Engineering, Addison-Wesley Publishing Company, Inc., 1975.

Johnson, J. R., "A Working Measure of Productivity," Datamation, February 1977, pp. 106-111.

Nolan, Richard L. and McFarlan, Warren F., "Effective EDP Project Management," Managing the Data Resource Function, West Publication Co., 1974, pp. 293-307.

CHAPTER SIX

PROGRAM TESTING

This chapter addresses testing. After presenting a testing report, an attempt is made to quantify the value of online programming with a tool like TSO (IBM's Time Sharing Option) which provides online compile and debug facilities (SPF, Structured Program Facility). Also, an unrealistic but actual software justification is presented to illustrate how not to justify software aids. Last, testing metrics from a large project are presented as a basis for continued analysis.

6.1 TESTING REPORTS AND SYSTEM TEST

Figure 6.1 summarizes the test jobs submitted by a programming group during a one-month period. Backing up this summary is an Individual Detail Level Report which lists all jobs submitted by each individual in a similar format. By reviewing the reports, testing exceptions are noted. Obviously, tests with high resource utilization are many times a function of testing requirements. Conversely, high costs may indicate poor testing and/or programming procedures. Also, the test reports provide individuals with comparative information on their testing habits. It is surprising how testing procedures improve when a feedback report exists.

When introducing the reports, you might consider the following awards:

1. Most Jobs Run
2. Highest Average Cost per Run
3. Greatest Job Charge
4. Fewest Jobs Run
5. Lowest Average Cost

Again, the recipients may or may not have performed well (more information is necessary) but more attention will be paid to testing in the future.

Having a well thought-out test plan is a desirable goal. Unfortunately, the definition of a good or bad plan is dependent on a subjective interpretation of a few basic rules:

1. Are the test objectives clearly established?
2. Will the transactions adequately test the desired logic plan?
3. Are the results predicted and documented?

Each test plan is unique, but if they follow the above basic rules, a good plan will result.

A comment on planning a system test is also appropriate. Normal work plan and Gantt chart techniques suffer deficiencies in the system test because the nature of the work tends to be group rather than individual, more interfaces exist, and the number of unknown tasks is dependent on the problems encountered.

No specific guidelines exist for planning a system test. The best procedure is to reference similar projects and estimate based on experience. Estimating in terms of elapsed time is recommended.

FOR THE PERIOD   FEB   1979

MANAGER - TAVELLA   SECTION MANAGER - JOHNSON

PROGRAMMER	TOTAL OCCUPNCY TIME (HRS.HUN)	TOTAL CPU TIME (HRS.HUN)	AVG TURN-AROUND TIME	CORE USED-LARGEST STEP	TOTAL LINES PRINTED LOCAL	TOTAL LINES PRINTED REMOTE	TOTAL TAPE & DISK I/O	TOTAL NUMBR OF JOBS	AVERAGE JOB CHARGE	TOTAL JOB CHARGE
BROOK, DENNIS	4.053	.391	1.54	1148	5307	95638	157084	243	$ 1.02	$ 248.54
SCHEMMEL, JIM	.008	.000	6.81	256	0	382	2	2	$ .34	$ .68
RIEKE, OTTO	.077	.003	.28	228	180	0	486	5	$ .30	$ 1.52
OESTERLY, PAUL	2.366	.985	4.89	844	3600	397842	728810	133	$ 6.14	$ 816.65
PETERSON, WES	5.938	1.072	.87	1163	35690	426403	214598	215	$ 3.95	$ 857.16
RICHARDSON, BOB	2.483	.365	3.29	1304	354	86858	419142	100	$ 3.30	$ 330.40
PURSEL, RON	6.284	.931	1.10	1532	6364	570758	247489	248	$ 2.61	$ 647.30
ROBINSON, JOHN	1.364	.307	11.22	1204	4330	94487	179777	79	$ 7.32	$ 578.81
BRINK, JOHN	2.053	.480	.59	1172	106	131965	84060	77	$ 3.26	$ 251.21
DUNFORD, RANDY	8.222	.961	1.53	3156	14457	131904	320555	210	$ 2.53	$ 531.48
ENGLE, BILL	4.940	.349	1.66	1296	41122	76268	66823	220	$ .99	$ 219.72
TUTTLE, TIM	9.420	.890	3.64	1456	4052	290051	292241	326	$ 1.74	$ 570.10
JUAREZ, KAREN	3.186	.883	2.64	1344	31942	467465	158454	252	$ 2.30	$ 560.73
MCCALE, BETH	4.083	.505	1.70	2512	17751	105648	142906	200	$ 1.48	$ 297.45
COLBY, GREG	.941	.063	4.00	1168	511	20829	11843	59	$ .74	$ 43.75
GAROUTTE, RON	9.019	.629	.56	1716	79060	82218	134455	279	$ 1.37	$ 384.65
HALER, LYNN	2.031	.123	.63	1152	21686	21726	36468	103	$ .83	$ 85.72
KOHATZ, LES	10.061	4.186	4.00	1188	159599	127250	709564	234	$ 7.33	$ 1715.91
HANKS, JANET	2.857	.304	3.15	1216	0	186490	74881	146	$ 1.51	$ 221.47
SOLOMON, STEVE	3.523	.957	.96	2000	2257	22813	26319	63	$ 4.60	$ 289.93
SCHAUER, JOE	2.976	.483	3.28	1328	17	137638	192775	133	$ 2.14	$ 285.37
GASFER, BOB	.113	.083	2.15	640	9926	74595	17487	22	$ 3.45	$ 75.97
BANKS, RICHARD	5.697	.760	3.40	1192	239515	70521	107991	252	$ 2.14	$ 541.19
DAVISON, JERRY	.754	.135	1.00	1140	7292	75182	29582	51	$ 2.99	$ 152.49
ADAMS, LEONARD	1.363	.322	6.03	1156	65538	137610	57016	110	$ 2.37	$ 261.18
SM TOTALS	93.812	16.167			750656	3832841	4410808	3762		$ 9989.38

SM TOTALS   3762 JOBS

AVG # OF STEPS -   1.58   AVG # OF PRINT LINES -   1218   AVG JOB CHG - $ 2.65   AVG TURNAROUND -   2.55

3464 JOBS SUBMITTED 8 AM THRU 5 PM - - - - 2885 JOBS - 83 %- TURNED IN 0-2 HRS   160 JOBS - 5 %- TURNED IN 2-4 HRS

100 JOBS - 3 %- TURNED IN 4-8 HRS   319 JOBS - 9 %- TURNED IN 8 + HRS

298 JOBS SUBMITTED 5 PM THRU 8 AM - - - - - AVERAGE TURNAROUND TIME -   2.38   167 JOBS HAD ZERO CPU TIME

Figure 6.1 Individual Testing Statistics

6.2 ONLINE PROGRAMMING

Intuitively, online job entry, online access to files, interactive debug, online compile, and editing functions are valuable assets to the programming profession; but how can this benefit be quantified?

The purpose of this topic is to quantify online programming tools such as IBM's TSO (Time Sharing Option) with the SPF (Structured Program Facility) option. Rather than generalize the logic, data has been extracted from an actual study. Using the material presented, the reader can adapt the approach for other environments. The organization is as follows:

> Classification of Test Time
> Quantifying the Value of Ideal Test Time
> Other Factors
> > a. Online Editing
> > b. Project Stage Relationship
> > c. Consistency/Availability
> > d. Costs
> Conclusion

Classification of Test Time

The classification of test turnaround on jobs (compiles, tests, etc.) is listed below.

Classification	Comment
Ideal: 1-15 minutes	Realized with TSO online compile and debug results in high productivity
Good: consistent conditions in which eight to sixteen runs are possible during the day per individual	This converts to 30-60 minute turnaround; time can be managed such that good productivity is possible
Fair: two hour turnaround	Fair turnaround is not acceptable on a continuing basis
Poor: more than two hour turnaround	Project scheduling is very difficult with poor turnarounds

One other relevant aspect of test turnaround is priority setting. For "hot" jobs on the critical path or jobs required for system test, a preferential scheme is generally used. Thus, even in fair to poor average times the few most critical jobs have been in the good range.

Quantifying the Value of Ideal Test Time

The environment of this analysis is a system development staff of about 130-135 personnel. Based on previous analysis of time allocation in the department, 36 percent of the staff's time was devoted to programming, testing, and resolving production problems. The remaining time was allocated to system design, administration, and miscellaneous activities. Since the department performed a variety of functions, the impact of ideal test time was related only to the programming and testing activities. The functions performed during these activities were:

> Submit and compile programs online
> Test programs interactively
> Test systems interactively
> Inquiry/list data sets online
> Build/change data sets online

The table below estimates the improvement of ideal test time (which implies online compile and debug) over good-fair test time.

	Nature of Work		
	Programming	Testing	Resolving Prod. Prob.
Percent of dept. time (36%)	18%	12%	6%
Portion of total budget (3M)	$540,000	360,000	180,000
Savings with ideal test time (estimated)	5%	50%	30%
Quantified savings	$27,000	180,000	54,000

Two conclusions can be drawn from this data. First, based on a $3 million department budget, the savings realized with ideal test turnaround is approximately $261,000. Second, since 36 percent of the department's time is devoted to the three activities, the productivity increase is 8.7 percent (.18 x .05 + .12 x .5 + .06 x .3). The savings come from reducing unproductive programming time through improved logistics, improved responsiveness, and undisrupted concentration periods.

Other Factors

A. Online Editing

The impact of slow response time for Systems Development personnel is no different than other divisional personnel using CRTs to perform a function. If response time exceeds the natural relax time of one to two seconds, individuals are idle for the remaining time.

Statistics on Systems Development response time for online editing functions are automatically recorded and show an average response time of 3.0 seconds with standard deviation of 2.1 seconds. Thus, assume that on 50 percent of the transactions, two seconds is lost time. Systems Development and Systems Software enter approximately 650,000 transactions a month. This,

$$2 \text{ sec.} \times 325,000 \; \frac{\text{Trans}}{\text{Month}} \times \frac{\text{Hr.}}{3600 \text{ sec.}} \times \frac{\$12}{\text{Hr.}} = \frac{\$2,166}{\text{Month}}$$

B. Project Stage Relationship

Depending on the project stage, delays will occur as test time deteriorates. The delay resulting from poor test turnaround may range from minimal to the worst situation: a direct relationship.

The system testing phase provides the best example of a direct relationship between test turnaround and elapsed time. If forty total runs are required for system test, and if four runs can be made in a day, then the elapsed time will be ten days. Consider the impact of dropping the average system test runs from four to two per day, because of poor test time. The contention is that the elapsed time would double; i.e., a direct relationship exists. If checking out system test results required a significant amount of time, say one day, then slower turnaround would have less than a direct relation to elapsed time. Thus, project schedules could be condensed with better test time, which means more work could be done. This allows the company to take advantage of system "opportunities" sooner.

C. Consistency/Availability

Consistency is also a key concept in any discussion of test time. Without a relatively stable testing environment, individuals are not able to plan their work. When production problems occur and production runs into or through the day, testing is impacted dramatically. Individuals arrive eager to accomplish productive work and the machine is not available.

D. Cost

Is online programming free? Assume 40 CRTs are required for a rental of $48,000 per year (40 x $1,200/year = $48,000). In regard to CPU resources, there may be no extra cost, assuming a virtual operating system. Some say online programming systems require less resources than batch, due to more efficient allocation of data sets, job overhead, less printed output, etc. In any case, the CPU resources may be an even tradeoff.

Conclusion

The methods of quantifying the value of ideal test time produce the following results:

A.	Ideal Testing	$261,000/yr.
B.	Online Editing $2,166/mo. or	$ 25,992/yr.

Both quantifying techniques are "inexact" macro approaches, but the direct benefits of ideal test time are no doubt in the $300,000 range. It is important to note that the comparison was based on good-to-fair versus ideal turnaround. The benefits increase when compared with poor turnaround.

A descriptive way of stating this dollar value is the word idleness - better test turnaround prevents idle time. Obviously, personnel are assigned to multiple tasks, but there are times when groups of individuals rely almost exclusively on test turnaround.

In Chapter Two, on the LOC/manday productivity chart, the percent improvement of online programming was stated as 15 percent for the implementation phase. This analysis concluded that the savings ranged from 5 percent to 50 percent depending on the activity (programming, testing, and resolving production problems).

Basically, the two conclusions are in agreement. If the implementation phase is 60 percent of a project and the total savings is 8.7 percent, then the savings for implementation is 14.5 percent. Remove the time for resolving production problems, which is not a developmental function, and a figure of around 15 percent is derived.

Two other benefits of improved turnaround which were not quantified are: 1) schedule condensing (reflected indirectly in the $261,000 above), and 2) improvement of morale.

Fred Brooks was once asked why he hadn't discussed test time availability in <u>Mythical Man-Month,</u> and whether he found it important. He responded by stating, "For programming projects test time is a necessity. If you don't have it, buy it."

The net result of the benefits can be reflected in two ways: same size staff accomplishing more, or a smaller staff accomplishing the work of today's staff. In other words, personnel are more effective. Eliminating idle time is a major benefit of ideal test time.

6.3 SOFTWARE JUSTIFICATION: HOW NOT TO

The reader might enjoy a naive cost justification study. The software package is a test data generator, and the information was extracted from an actual study. The company and author must remain anonymous for obvious reasons. Also, the software package is not mentioned by name.

The following cost justification facts and figures were presented:

1. Estimated Machine Savings

   An average reduction of 50 percent of the machine units expenditure is anticipated, due to the following:

   a) Smaller test files as opposed to large "live" data files

   b) More meaningful test data

   c) Expediting testing the changes associated with production programs

   d) Reduction of reruns based on more complete testing.

   Estimated Annual Savings $303,573.00

2. Estimated Manpower Savings

   Manpower expenditure reductions are estimated at 30 percent, but could very well be higher. This percentage takes into account the following:

   a) Increased programmer and system analyst productivity by decreasing the number of "test shots"

   b) A significant reduction in time spent coding test data

   c) Increased productivity by eliminating the time spent waiting for test tapes to be mounted during terminal sessions

   d) A significant reduction in programmer "debug" time expended due to inadequate test data.

   Estimated Annual Savings $110,940.00

Payback

Installation charge is $8,500 with a yearly rental of $350 plus a 10 percent maintenance charge. Let's see what payback would result from this investment:

$$\text{Payback (years)} = \frac{\text{Development Cost}}{\text{Benefits} - \text{Operating Cost}}$$

$$= \frac{\$8,500}{(303,573 + 110,940) - (350 + 35)}$$

$$= \frac{\$8,500}{\$414,513 - 385} = \frac{\$8,500}{\$414,128}$$

$$= .020525 \text{ years or } 7.5 \text{ days!}$$

Not a bad return.

What is the Problem?

A commendable approach, but the savings for both machine utilization and test hours are simply unreasonable. Those using the test data generators know that in a few situations, say 5 percent, the above savings can result. In other situations, it is advantageous to use "live" files for data passed from one program to another, or user generated data, etc. Also, as with any software package, training time is required. Thus, the yearly benefits would be less than $20,100 (5% x $414,513), and produce a payback of six to twelve months, which is conceivable for a well-designed software package.

6.4 TESTING METRICS

There exist few published statistics on test resources used for projects. The data presented in Figure 6.2 was extracted from an automated system (KOMAND) which logged statistics for programming members on the project teams and the data is considered accurate.

This testing data is only a first step toward quantifying test statistics. Unfortunately, the data is not detailed by compiles, unit tests, ancillary runs, and system tests; but, as project metrics they provide a basis and framework for future analysis.

Characteristics of the Marketing Information System (MIS) and Product Data Base (PDB) projects were documented in Chapter Two, Section Three - Project History. The third project was labeled Everyday Upgrade (EDU). It was a twenty manyear effort which upgraded a large order processing system from a 7074 machine to the 370. This includes completely restructuring and condensing the master files. About 60 percent of the coding was on new programs with the balance of the effort devoted to modifying existing programs. Comprising the project team were thirteen individuals, nine of whom wrote programs during implementation. The following productivity techniques were used on EDU: module programming, HIPO, Top-Down Development, structured programming, team operation, online librarian, and some structured diagrams.

Reviewing the summary testing metrics, Figure 6.3, it is concluded that an individual in the implementation phase submits between nine and thirteen jobs per day. The CPU metrics vary considerably based on the nature of the project. For example, MIS and EDU were tested with large volume of production data so CPU usage is high. Another interesting statistic is the number of tests required per ten verbs: it ranged from 4.9 to 8.1. This means that if a project were estimated at 5,000 verbs, the tests required would fall in the range of 2,500 to 4,050. And last, for budgeting purposes at a macro level, the charge per day per person falls in the $20-40 range.

MONTH	TOTAL JOBS SUBMITTED			CPU HOURS			$ COST		
	EDU	MIS	PDB	EDU	MIS	PDB	EDU	MIS	PDB
1.	1,058			3.1			4,621		
2.	1,341		645	3.0		1.0	3,335		596
3.	1,418		1,166	4.9		4.1	4,346		2,066
4.	1,503	365	1,503	4.3	.1	3.5	2,819	399	2,315
5.	1,613	1,597	1,747	4.9	3.5	3.7	3,059	2,450	2,995
6.	2,157	1,147	2,908	11.9	5.3	2.4	11,012	3,259	2,418
7.	2,255	1,393	2,479	11.4	7.4	2.6	12,832	4,911	2,454
8.	2,197	1,306	1,610	12.4	23.5	2.1	13,006	12,259	1,754
9.	2,466	1,274	2,461	19.6	28.3	5.7	16,007	12,625	5,433
10.	2,184	2,053	2,145	16.5	21.6	5.8	14,299	12,117	5,335
TOT.	18,192	9,135	16,664	92.0	89.7	30.9	85,336	48,020	25,366

Figure 6.2 Detail Metrics

AVERAGES	EDU	MIS	PDB
Jobs/Day	90.96	65.25	92.58
Jobs/Person/Day	10.11	9.32	13.23
CPU Min/Person/Month	61.33	108.98	29.43
Job Charge/Person/Day	$47.41	$49.00	$20.13
Test/10 Verbs	Unknown	4.90	8.10
PROJECT ATTRIBUTES	EDU	MIS	PDB
Implementation Mandays	200	140	180
Staffing Level	9	7	7
Number of Verbs	Unknown	18,500	20,493

Figure 6.3 Summary Metrics

PART II

CHAPTER SIX DISCUSSION QUESTIONS

SECTION

6.1   1.   Can peer pressure be used to influence testing procedures?

6.2   2.   If batch turnaround on test jobs were five minutes or less via an RJE terminal, would many of the benefits of TSO software be reduced?

6.4   3.   Testing metrics can be used for hardware resource estimating, but are there other uses?

BIBLIOGRAPHY

Brooks, Frederick P., Jr., <u>The Mythical Man-Month Essays on Software Engineering</u>, Addison-Wesley Publishing Company, Inc., 1975.

PART III

MAINTENANCE PRODUCTIVITY

"A PROGRAMMER NOW COSTS THE SAME AS A SMALL 370"
IBM Salesman

PART III

MAINTENANCE PRODUCTIVITY

No one will argue that maintenance (used synonymously with support) will always be with us, and that it is expensive. In order to manage support, the unique aspects of the task must be identified. Basically, the support function is concerned with managing the following:

      Enhancements (user requests)
      Production problems
      Support personnel (burnout)
      System documentation
      Transition from development
      Program and system efficiency

These general topics are covered in Chapters Seven and Eight. Although some overlap exists, Chapter Seven presents an integrated plan for managing the manager. Specifically, Chapter Seven explains how to quantify four objectives which can be used to monitor the maintenance manager's performance. The numerical values illustrated may sound unreasonable, but establishing a positive trend and noting deviations from the plan is the relevant point. Two of the objectives are based on LOC, one on the application of the burnout theory, and the fourth on enhancement performance. Data from an existing organization is used to demonstrate the procedure.

Chapter Eight provides tools for the support manager (who is being managed in Chapter Seven) to improve productivity. They are as follows:

      Documentation
      Language Selection
      Project Monitoring Software Packages
      System Optimization
      Post Implementation Audit
      Selecting the Portfolio
      Report Design

CHAPTER SEVEN *

QUANTIFYING MAINTENANCE PERFORMANCE

It is the end of the year 198X. Joe is the manager of a relatively large Data Processing Support Organization (staff of forty). Major development (large projects exceeding 100 mandays) is performed in a separate organization. The context of the dialogue is Joe's yearly performance review. Names have been changed to protect the innocent.

Boss: Joe, I'm not too satisfied with your performance this year.

Joe: I know things haven't worked out well this year, but a number of unanticipated problems have occurred.

Boss: At the beginning of the year, we mutually agreed to improve in four areas, and we subsequently established four objectives.

Joe: I think the organization did well by meeting 80 percent of our schedule dates and only experiencing a 5 percent turnover.

Boss: Let's talk about the specific objectives one at a time.

Joe: Okay.

Boss: The first goal was to increase the LOC (lines of code) supported per individual by 2 percent while providing the same user support on enhancements. Today, the staff exceeds that of last year's.

Joe: I know it looks bad, but the documentation of two or three of those old systems is not adequate. It is hard for my people to be productive on antiquated systems.

Boss: The second objective was to reduce by 3 percent the number of production problems (per 100,000 LOC), and reduce the average time spent on each problem. In both cases, no change was noted.

Joe: The extra production problems recently have been extra tough. Furthermore, my expert was on vacation twice when his system was down for three days.

Boss: The next goal was to rotate individuals such that the average time on a given system is less than three years. According to the recent audit, the average increased from 2.9 years to 3.1 years.

Joe: The average increase of 0.2 isn't much. Besides, I didn't feel my people wanted to change, and I didn't want to create morale problems.

Boss: The last objective was to complete user requests within budgeted time (plus or minus 15 percent), and within the scheduled elapsed time (plus or minus 25 percent). Performance in this area was very good.

_____

*Adapted from Johnson, Monitoring Programming Performance, pp. 18-22.

Joe: Right, I view this as an important aspect of the job. Eighty percent of the time, my staff was exactly on target.

Now, about my raise . . .

A similar dialogue may not take place in many organizations today, but a strong tendency does exist to manage by quantifiable objectives. In order to improve performances, objectives have to be established. Establishing objectives implies measurement.

This chapter explains the purpose of four selected objectives (Figure 7.1), provides the definitional groundwork necessary to obtain supporting data, and presents examples from a commercial applications environment. Over time, the objectives should improve performance; thus, the individual merits are the central issues. After explaining the logic supporting these four objectives, the tools required to quantify the data will be presented along with actual data.

THE OBJECTIVES

A. Increase the LOC supported per individual by 2 percent while providing the same level of support on enhancements.

B. Reduce by 3 percent the number of production problems (per 100,000 LOC), and the time spent on each production problem.

C. Rotate individuals such that the average time on a given system is less than three years.

D. Complete user enhancement requests within budgeted time (plus or minus 15 percent), and within scheduled elapsed time (plus or minus 25 percent).

Figure 7.1 Four Performance Objectives

Objective One

"Increase the LOC supported per individual by 2 percent while providing the same level of support on enhancements."

Work falls into one of three categories: enhancement, must-do, and administration. This objective assumes that performance for these activities can be improved; i.e., the same work can be performed by a smaller staff. In this context, the objective could result in a manpower budget reduction or a shift of resources to the enhancement area. The second part of the objective reflects a management decision that the manpower devoted to enhancement work is adequate and manpower reduction is preferred. Management actions which may accomplish this objective are improved planning, design, and documentation; note that objectives do not define how to accomplish the improvement - that is the job of the manager.

Knowledge of production software and personnel allocation provides the basis for the first objective - reducing the support staff. Data is obtained through analysis of LOC and time reporting. An example will be presented after examining the merits of the other three objectives.

Objective Two

"Reduce by three percent the number of production problems (per 100,000 LOC) and the time spent on each production problem."

One aspect of must-do maintenance is resolving production problems. This objective motivates activities which will reduce these problems. For example, it may impel stricter validating rules or establishment of more control on program changes. When problems do occur, the average resolution time reflects the quality, knowledge, and training of the staff. Again, the objective does not state how to improve the staff. This objective necessitates information from two areas - lines of code and production problem statistics.

Objective Three

"Rotate individuals such that the average time on a given system is less than three years."

This objective is based on the belief that planned job rotation is one of the best techniques available to provide training, job enrichment, and subsequently insure a healthy organization.

What are the by-products of this objective? First, it assures adequate documentation. Knowing a system has only temporary "ownership" means that providing reliable documentation is a necessity. Individuals are self-motivated to improve the documentation so a complete package can be passed on to their successors. Second, planned rotations promote productivity by providing a continuing challenge or learning opportunity. Third, changing assignments broadens an individual's base of experience. Both the second and third by-products are techniques of obtaining greater job enrichment. Assuring back-up experience in emergency situations is the fourth favorable impact of this objective. Thus this one objective, "job rotation on the average of every three years," results in benefits both to the individual and the corporation.

Objective Three is the simplest to monitor, but one of the most difficult to implement. A one-hour review of personnel assignments every six months accomplishes the monitoring. Implementation is, of course, a management action. It requires thoughtful planning and careful consideration of personnel strengths and weaknesses. Also, human nature is such that new challenges do not always look so encouraging when one is comfortably situated in a position. This applies to managers as well as programmers. In brief, enforcing this one simple objective accomplishes many others as a by-product.

Objective Four

"Complete user enhancement requests within budgeted time (plus or minus 15 percent) and within scheduled elapsed time (plus or minus 25 percent)."

Controlling the enhancement classification of work is the result of this objective. The ample percentage allowance of error exists for two reasons: 1) production problems may interrupt progress on enhancements, and 2) insisting on performance too close to budget may produce adverse effects; i.e., compromises on performing the work as it should be done. Predicting completion dates is not a purely analytical process, and, if dates become the paramount issue, a net loss results.

Objective Two guards against insufficient testing that might result from cutting corners. However, note that reducing production problems (Objective Two) may conflict with installing user enhancements within budget and on time (Objective Four). An optimal solution involves progressive performance improvements in both areas rather than absolute perfection for one objective. A time reporting system is appropriate for recording estimated hours, actual hours, scheduled dates, and completion dates.

HOW TO MONITOR THE STATED OBJECTIVES

Establishing objectives which will improve performance has been the subject of this section up to this point. The question now is, "What measurement data must be collected to support the objectives, and what recording tools are required?"

Information pertinent to the objective requires quantitative knowledge of the following:

1. Production software
2. Personnel resources allocation
3. Production problems
4. Personnel assignments

Obtaining data on the last item is straightforward. It was covered in the discussion of Objective Three (personnel rotation).

The remainder of this section explains the definitional groundwork and tools required to implement Objectives One, Two, and Four. The data presented is from a commercial applications environment.

PRODUCTION SOFTWARE DEFINITION AND EXAMPLE

Knowledge of software means analyzing and understanding the existing production programs in an installation. For example, is the environment 500,000 LOC or 5,000,000 LOC; one programming language or multiple languages; 100 percent batch or a mixture of batch and online; average program size - 500 LOC or 1,000 LOC?

To illustrate the type of analysis required to answer these questions, a recent study will be explained. Figure 7.2 lists the results of the analysis. As the chart indicates, the batch programs comprised 95 percent of the total LOC with online code accounting for the other five percent. In addition, all programs were commercial applications (versus scientific, operating systems), written in three main languages: COBOL (80 percent), PL1 (17 percent), MARK IV (2 percent), and other (1 percent).

The purpose of the study was to accurately count and classify LOC for the major production systems. Special programs were written to match the Librarian File (Source Code Storage) to the production library. If a module resided in both libraries, it was selected for analysis. The time required for design, programming and analysis totaled 300 hours or approximately $3,000. Another $1,300 was used for executing the programs.

LOC IN THOUSANDS

Production System	Online	Batch	Total	Number CICS Programs	Number Batch Programs
Financial Reporting	0	99	99	0	138
Inventory Control	0	204	204	0	168
Release Monitoring	2	64	66	1	63
Cost Management	0	52	52	0	36
Cost Accounting	0	35	35	0	54
Premanufacturing	2	118	120	1	149
Production Planning	7	136	143	23	78
Ten Miscellaneous	7	150	157	14	339
Accounts Receivable	14	55	69	27	79
Billing	6	68	74	0	87
Name & Address	19	27	46	65	32
Season	1	135	136	1	281
Everyday	0	159	159	0	351
Marketing	6	267	273	16	488
Research	0	68	68	0	90
Employee Information	0	181	181	0	241
Accounts Payable	29	46	75	108	45
TOTALS	93	1,864	1,957	256	2,719

Summary Analysis

Batch: Number of Programs   2,719 $\frac{LOC}{PGM}$ = 686
      Number of LOC   1,864,000

Online: Number of Programs   256 $\frac{LOC}{PGM}$ = 363
      Number of LOC   93,000

TOTAL
  Number of Programs   2,975 $\frac{LOC}{PGM}$ = 658
  Number of LOC   1,957,000

PER PERSON (with overhead)
  Total LOC   1,957,000 $\frac{LOC}{PERSON}$ = 48,925
  Number on Staff   40

Figure 7.2 LOC Analysis

The results of the study showed the production for 2,975 programs totaled about 2,000,000 L O C. The average size program in the batch environment was twice the average for the online programs (686 L O C batch vs. 363 L O C online) (Figure 7.2).

Since the maintenance staff supporting the systems consisted of forty programmers, the average L O C per person was slightly less than 50,000. This average has meaning within a company, but is extremely dependent on definitions and the nature or type of support activities. L O C is defined as all source statements. It includes internal comments and job control statements.

ALLOCATION OF HUMAN RESOURCES

Objectives in the support environment are integral to the allocation of individuals' time. A significant difference may exist between minimum support staffing and the actual support staff. To analyze the activities further, a series of definitions is required.

Support activities are divided into three areas:

1. Administrative overhead
2. Repair, fix-it-if-it-breaks, and must-do maintenance
3. Enhancements, improvements, new developments.

Minimal production support is, of course, both 1 and 2 above. Depending on the volume of enhancements, the support level can vary significantly. The definitions presented are arbitrary.

The administrative overhead time category is, for the most part, nondiscretionary. On an average, the percent of administrative overhead is relatively constant. Administrative time is not related to a user request. Education, vacation, and sick leave are examples of administrative time.

The second support activity is must-do maintenance. As the name indicates, it is time which D P has little or no control over. It includes time allocated to resolve hardware, operational and software abnormal terminations (abends). Unusual Condition Reports (U C Rs) always result when this time is recorded. Also, must-do maintenance results from a change in corporate directions, new federal regulation, or interface requirements (for example, new tax laws), and last, time spent with the user discussing questions or potential requests prior to the offical establishment of a request.

Enhancements result from user requests for system modification. Work in this area includes efficiency or reporting modifications, new applications or subsystems, and adding additional functions to an existing system. Historic knowledge of the time devoted to each of these areas is required prior to establishing meaningful objectives. Obviously, the most straightforward way to obtain data is from a time recording system: in one commercial environment, 30 percent of the resources are devoted to administrative time, 26 percent for must-do activities, and 44 percent to enhancements.

Subtracting time for enhancements and a portion of administrative time produces a theoretical maximum L O C/person double the 48,925, or approxiamtely 100,000. However, there is obviously a danger point where must-do maintenance is jeopardized. Backup, training, and commitment to user enhancements are all important and vary by organization. Also, on a system by system basis, the LOC/person may vary depending on the system's complexity and priority.

PRODUCTION PROBLEMS

The question is not whether a DP system will fail, but rather how often the system will fail. Generally, failures are called abends (abnormal endings). They can be due to hardware errors, disk space, OS failures, data entry, JCL, and, of course, program bugs. The emphasis for systems support is with program-caused abends. Controlling and reporting production problems can be handled by a UCR (Unusual Condition Report) form (see 9.1 Unusual (Error) Conditions). All data concerning the error condition is recorded and maintained for reference.

A detailed procedure is required to adequately locate the source and cause of production problems. Assuming a procedure is available, worthwhile metrics are produced by relating abends back to systems and LOC. What are some meaningful relationships which can be computed using program caused abend data? Consider the following:

1. Average abends per total LOC
2. Average abends by system
3. Average time to correct problem in total and by system

This information is not difficult to obtain, and probably exists in most organizations today. The two million lines of code discussed previously abend due to program problems - between thirty and forty times per month. Assuming an average system is 100,000 LOC, the abend rate falls in the range of 1.5 to 2 abends per month. Factors such as system age, run frequency, and rate of modification (change) all contribute to a variance from the average. A simple plot of abends by major system or area of responsibility is the tool for establishing production problem objectives.

CONCLUSION

This section attempts to establish pragmatic performance measurements for the manager of a support organization. Developing these basic management objectives requires minor acquisition costs. The key is consistent definitions and selecting objectives which improve the overall efficiency of the organization. The particular objectives established here may not apply to all organizations. If not, others can be established. For example:

Test Time Budget
Reducing Administrative Time
Response Time to User Enhancements
Personnel Turnover

It is important to remember that overemphasis on any given objective can produce undesirable results. People will attempt to meet any predefined objective they are monitored against. In many instances, objectives conflict with each other. In these situations, an optimal solution is not identical to maximizing each objective.

Setting and monitoring objectives within an organization is more straightforward than comparing one organization to another. The confusion results from lack of consistent definition. If the industry used standardized time reporting systems and L O C definitions, significant progress would be made toward a more scientific management of the support activities.

Well thought-out objectives do not dictate how a manager gets results. They allow a manager to use ingenuity to accomplish the goals. The objectives were set at a macro level to monitor the performance of the manager.

PART III

CHAPTER SEVEN DISCUSSION QUESTIONS

1. Are the objectives stated more indicative of management performance than LOC would be for a programmer?

2. When speaking in terms of programmer maintenance support (manpower/LOC), does LOC have meaning at the program level?

SUGGESTED READING

Peeples, Donald E., "Measure for Productivity," Datamation, May 1978, pp. 222-230.

BIBLIOGRAPHY

Johnson, J. R., "Monitoring Programming Performance," Journal of Systems Management, June 1978, pp. 18-22.

CHAPTER EIGHT

MANAGEMENT TECHNIQUES FOR MAINTENANCE

This chapter discusses a variety of management issues relating to productivity in the support environment. Figure 8.1 illustrates the relationship between the seven topics, (documentation, language selection, software project monitoring packages, system optimization, post implementation audit, selecting portfolio, and report design) to internal and external DP interfaces. The first five productivity techniques apply within the DP division, while selecting portfolio and report design are related to external DP interfaces. Selecting projects for a portfolio requires a ranking and quantifying procedure to support "feelings" about the appropriate direction; the political atmosphere is obviously of importance. The procedure is appropriate for the larger (25-100 manday) maintenance efforts and also developmental projects (100 plus mandays), which were the subject of Part II. Using a "bad example" of report design is the method of presentation for the latter topic. Individual productivity aids presented in Chapters One and Two also apply in the maintenance or support mode.

A.	Management of Support	B.	User Interface
	1. Documentation	6.	Selecting Portfolio
	2. Language Selection	7.	Report Design
	3. Software Project Monitoring Package		
	4. System Optimization		
	5. Post Implementation Audits		

Figure 8.1 Topic Relationships

8.1 DOCUMENTATION

There are a few basic premises about documentation:

1. No one has developed the ideal form of documentation.

2. Individuals will not voluntarily maintain documentation. Thus, after appropriate documentation is established, there is only one sure way of maintaining its accuracy: provide audit controls.

3. During a project's development, various documents are prepared and used to facilitate communication, provide training, and define system capabilities. When the project is implemented, the functional purpose of the majority of these documents comes to an end. Attempting to use them as maintenance documentation is not wise.

4. The English language is still an acceptable means of documentation.

5. The best program documentation is well written code with descriptive comments.

6. Secondary program documentation, like structure charts, sounds theoretically worthwhile. But, from a practical standpoint, maintenance is the problem. The program coding has to be modified for changes. Why force dual documentation and effort by requiring structure charts?

7. The basic maintenance documentation is:
   System Narrative
   Program Narrative (not more than one to two pages)
   System Flowchart
   Record Layouts
   Field Descriptions
   Report Descriptions
   Program Listing
   JCL
   Index

The recommended method of maintaining documentation is with a documentation library facility. The library consists of physical facilities for storing documentation, and a librarian who, in addition to controlling the distribution of the material, audits for completeness.

It is easy to argue against a documentation library:

Extra operating expense
Physical area not available
Potential bottleneck (nonaccessibility)
Duplicate sets will exist
One-time construction costs

But, the fact of the matter is that a documentation library and associated staff is one of the best investments possible. No other approach is more effective for improving documentation accuracy and accessibility. If a documentation library is not a possibility, the next best approach is periodic, independent audits with reports to management.

8.2 LANGUAGE SELECTION

When analyzing language efficiency and selection, it is convenient to present the two extremes - Assembler language and report generators. Contrary to popular opinion, Assembler language shops are not always efficient or effective. True, less core storage is required, but overall throughput and total costs are the issues. At a macro level, throughput is composed of two factors:

1. Effectiveness - Resources expended on development, enhancements, and maintenance

2. Efficiency - Execution efficiency of computer programs.

The common programming languages (COBOL, FORTRAN, PL1, BASIC) win point one without much competition from Assembler. The impression that a commercial Assembler shop enjoys execution efficiency is based on over-emphasizing the value of core storage and assuming all Assembler programs are efficient. To counter this impression, consider that 1) core is no longer as expensive as it once was, and 2) generating superfluous code is simply too easy. The typical commercial programmer does not have the expertise to consistently write efficient code and subsequently modify the code so it executes efficiently. Leave Assembler language to the gifted few who develop operating systems, high level compilers, and I/O routines.

To most, high level languages are thought of as report generations; for example, using MARK IV (Informatics) is one of the most expeditious means of generating impromptu reports. But, do not be fooled by the salesman who claims MARK IV is ideal for all types (validates, updates, and general use) of processing. It can be a disaster for systems that are not simplistic in nature.

When the system specifications call for complex processing, programmers are forced to play tricks with the high level language to accomplish the objective. Since the documentation is about 25 percent as detailed as that provided for by COBOL, FORTRAN, or PL1, the benefits become negative - it takes longer to debug, documentation is difficult, and processing times are two to three times longer than necessary.

High-level languages save significant time for those straightforward extract, sort, summarize, and list jobs. In 2.2, a 10 percent overall productivity gain was estimated for using report generators. But, do not attempt to program a major system or you will regret it.

8.3 PROJECT MONITORING SOFTWARE PACKAGES

The following is a quote from an IBM advertisement letter:

> If you need help in completing projects on time, within budget,
> and to specification, you'll want to read this letter and the
> enclosed brochure. They include important facts about two IBM
> program products that can help you in your role as project
> manager - control, time, resources and costs. Both program
> products contain a set of routines that can guide you in defining
> project objectives, developing comprehensive plans, identifying
> critical work activities, and tracking resources. What's more,
> these versatile products offer you the flexibility you need to
> alter plans to reflect everchanging conditions. They can give
> fast answers to "what if . . .?" questions concerning alternative
> courses of action.

This section attempts to place project monitoring software packages in perspective as a productivity tool, and as it relates to PERT/CPM and project simulation.

Automated systems perform three basic objectives:

1. Time reporting
2. Generating PERT/CPM networks
3. Simulating alternatives

Figure 8.2 lists the inputs required for each of the objectives.

INPUT REQUIREMENTS

	Input Required	Reporting	PERT/ CPM	Simulation
1.	Task Definitions	Y	Y	Y
2.	Task Durations	Y	Y	Y
3.	Task Relationships	N	Y	Y
4.	Task Completions	Y	Y	Y
5.	Control Parameters	N	Y	Y
6.	Individual Skills	N	N	Y
7.	Task Priorities	N	N	Y
8.	Task Costs	N	N	Y

Figure 8.2 Software Package Inputs

The objective of a time reporting system is one or all of the following: computing charges for services, improving estimates via accurate history, and defining work so involved parties have a common understanding of the tasks. Time spent on tasks can be applied daily, weekly or monthly, although weekly is the general rule. In addition to satisfying these objectives, time reporting is a basic step which normally precedes more elaborate planning, control, and scheduling.

Automated PERT/CPM networks are used when the manual effort to accomplish the clerical work is too costly or time consuming. However, if there are many changes, the manual effort to update the system can also be time consuming. Simulating the impact of adding or deleting tasks or projects to an existing schedule implies some form of automatic scheduling, which is generally a complex area. The output can provide management with alternatives for resource allocation, completion dates, manpower assignments, and critical path changes.

Of the total projects in the world, probably one-half of 1 percent make significant benefits possible by placing the entire project plan on an automated network. The effort to understand the project monitoring software package and maintain the data accuracy exceeds the benefits for most projects. However, this does not imply that planning on projects is optional. Planning is essential, but the point is that it can be accomplished without the burden of a complex automated system.

There are two overriding comments. First, the more a software package does, the more input is required. Second, there is no tool available which will guarantee the success of a maintenance or developmental project (see Chapter Four).

8.4 SYSTEM OPTIMIZATION

A number of techniques exist for optimizing run times of DP Systems/Programs. Tuning efforts generally concentrate on the following:

1. Compiler Optimizers
2. Improved Sort Packages
3. Larger Blocking Factors
4. Program Coding changes for efficiency.

Improvements from the above can be significant - up to 10-15% of total resources. But where does tuning effort start, and where are the bottlenecks? One existing software package provides the answers to these questions (Plan IV from Capex Corporation). Please see Figures 8.3 and 8.4.

What more can be requested? The report provides all-encompassing data on critical programs. By initiating tuning efforts with this base of information, a direction appropriate to solving the unique problems of an organization can be established.

```
*******************************************
*                                         *
*        C R I T I C A L   J O B S        *
*                                         *
*                  A N D                  *
*                                         *
*    C R I T I C A L   P R O G R A M S    *
*                                         *
*******************************************
```

THE FOLLOWING REPORTS SHOW THE 30 MOST
IMPORTANT OR CRITICAL PROGRAMS AND JOBS
IN VARIOUS CATEGORIES.

THE CRITICAL JOB REPORTS SHOWN ARE

1. LONGEST RUNNING.
2. MOST CPU TIME.
3. MOST DISK EXCPS.
4. MOST TAPE EXCPS.
5. MOST PRINT LINES.
6. HIGHEST PAGING RATE
7. MOST I/O BOUND.
8. MOST CPU BOUND.
9. MOST SERVICE UNITS.
10. CORRELATION REPORT.

THE CRITICAL PROGRAM REPORTS SHOWN ARE

1. MOST FREQUENTLY EXECUTED.
2. MOST TOTAL CPU TIME.
3. MOST AVERAGE CPU TIME.
4. MOST TOTAL DISK EXCPS.
5. MOST TOTAL TAPE EXCPS.
6. HIGHEST PAGING RATE.
7. MOST ABENDS.
8. MOST MAIN STORAGE USED.
9. MOST I/O BOUND.
10. MOST CPU BOUND.
11. MOST SERVICE UNITS.
12. CORRELATION REPORT.

LICENSED FROM CAPEX CORPORATION

PLAN IV

Figure 8.3 Performance Measures

ANALYSIS OF CRITICAL JOBS

** LONGEST RUNNING **

NO.	JOB NAME	ACCOUNTING FIELD	START DATE	START TIME	SERVICE UNITS(100S)	EXECUTION TIME	CPU TIME	EXCPS (100S) DISK	TAPE	RATE (PER CPU SEC) EXCPS	PAGING	LINES (100S)	PERCENTAGE CPU/EXEC	OF TOTAL	CUMUL TOTAL
1.	SC28LF25	0,7,080,150,	01/16/79	1013	1601	11.03.32	.01.19	143	0	181	179	23	0.1	0.5	0.5
2.	CR27U130	0001,0002.99	01/22/79	0821	4568	9.21.47	.02.41	107	0	66	124	134	0.4	0.4	1.0
3.	MI28E501	3,4,800,180,	01/18/79	1120	44439	6.58.44	.14.53	1510	40	174	82	239	3.5	0.3	1.4
4.	OR2SPBLK	0,5,7200,100	01/05/79	1041	53841	6.36.36	.24.24	5226	49	360	9	1	6.1	0.3	1.7
5.	OR2SPRLK	0,5,3600,999	01/11/79	1251	29254	6.03.46	1.00.04	4	0	0	9	9	16.5	0.3	2.0
6.	SC28LF25	0,7,080,150,	01/15/79	2030	1347	4.56.10	.00.57	143	0	252	28	23	0.3	0.2	2.3
7.	SY29LACC	0,2,9999,999	01/01/79	2111	36759	4.50.10	.11.51	1856	0	261	2	381	4.0	0.2	2.6
8.	MI24V550	0,6,9999,999	01/15/79	1347	38082	4.48.34	.24.38	140	284	29	7	2	8.5	0.2	2.8
9.	MI24V550	0,6,9999,999	01/18/79	0923	24447	4.28.22	.20.49	10	124	11	12	120	7.7	0.2	3.0
10.	OR27HCPY	0,5,3600,100	01/24/79	1213	24004	4.26.49	.18.18	0	1431	130	12	4	6.8	0.2	3.3
11.	SL24S17P	0,1,700,10,0	01/17/79	1441	38358	4.15.21	.13.24	2160	14	271	38	9	5.2	0.2	3.5
12.	CB29D170	0, ,4	01/22/79	1236	12104	4.09.59	.07.30	296	781	240	10	3	2.9	0.2	3.7
13.	MI24V190	0,6,9999,999	01/12/79	1352	30887	3.57.32	.19.32	48	793	72	7	32	8.2	0.2	3.9
14.	IM22FTSL	0,1,830,030,	01/02/79	1245	14635	3.52.57	.06.26	1912	12	499	15	0	2.7	0.2	4.1
15.	SY209TCT	0,2,9999,999	01/15/79	1213	10129	3.39.07	.07.00	1294	0	308	17	1	3.1	0.1	4.3
16.	MI24BU1H	0,1,1200,60,	01/04/79	2304	38887	3.31.01	.17.11	0	296	29	3	51	8.1	0.1	4.5
17.	MI24KU22	0,1,1200,50,	01/02/79	1036	46911	3.27.33	.14.34	2152	32	250	34	4	7.0	0.1	4.7
18.	MI24V190	0,6,9999,999	01/18/79	0948	21683	3.15.21	.18.27	59	684	67	14	34	9.4	0.1	4.9
19.	MI24BU40	0,1,900,20,0	01/09/79	1340	10573	3.14.28	.04.31	1112	13	415	50	0	2.3	0.1	5.0
20.	SL24SU17	0,1,700,10,0	01/16/79	1348	32325	3.09.57	.09.59	1926	14	324	45	34	5.2	0.1	5.2
21.	IE238RUL	0,5,045,005,	01/12/79	0910	1108	3.07.50	.00.33	1	159	482	9	0	0.2	0.1	5.4
22.	SC25K800	0,3,600,600	01/09/79	1223	15066	3.04.38	.07.42	100	56	34	33	32	4.1	0.1	5.5
23.	IM22FTSM	0,1,830,030,	01/17/79	1620	20328	3.02.04	.07.40	2579	5	562	8	4	4.2	0.1	5.7
24.	MI28E501	3,4,900,90,0	01/15/79	1431	11084	2.58.11	.13.34	79	1	10	8	1	7.6	0.1	5.8
25.	MI28E111	3,4,900,7,0	01/05/79	1705	17430	2.57.30	.09.57	1616	124	292	1	230	5.6	0.1	6.0
26.	MI24V520	0,6,9999,999	01/22/79	0043	133739	2.56.50	.39.53	1011	447	61	0	1	22.5	0.1	6.1
27.	MI24K530	0,1,9999,99	01/29/79	1810	119271	2.56.02	.38.50	698	254	41	1	2	22.0	0.1	6.3
28.	MI24V990	0,6,9999,99	01/11/79	0910	27556	2.54.09	.18.47		1039	92	9	9	10.7	0.1	6.4
29.	SL24S17P	0,1,500,10,0	01/10/79	0853	29756	2.51.42	.09.05	1990	11	367	39	23	5.2	0.1	6.6
30.	CW24Q50A	0,6,9999,999	01/04/79	1226	14526	2.50.09	.10.49	537	0	83	17	457	6.3	0.1	6.7

*** SUMMARY SHOWING RELATIVE IMPORTANCE ***

6.7 PER CENT OF TOTAL PROBLEM PROGRAM EXECUTION TIME
7.5 PER CENT OF TOTAL PROBLEM PROGRAM CPU TIME
8.0 PER CENT OF TOTAL PROBLEM PROGRAM DISK EXCPS
4.8 PER CENT OF TOTAL PROBLEM PROGRAM TAPE EXCPS
0.3 PER CENT OF TOTAL PROBLEM PROGRAM LINES PRINTED
5.8 PER CENT OF TOTAL PROBLEM PROGRAM PAGE-INS AND PAGE-OUTS
7.9 PER CENT OF TOTAL PROBLEM PROGRAM SERVICE UNITS

Figure 8.4 Longest Running Jobs

8.5 POST IMPLEMENTATION AUDIT

A post implementation audit serves two valuable functions. First, it formally assesses the success of a project, and second, the audit is the first step in preparing a system for the transition from development to support. Figure 8.5 provides an example post implementation audit checklist. From a project viewpoint, the emphasis would be on specific problems or successful techniques that might be helpful in future projects. For example, by comparing actual and estimated results, guidelines can be developed or improved for future projects. From a support viewpoint, the audit assures completion of the project. All audits should be filed in a central location accessible to all parties involved.

In Chapter 3, the project phases were defined as Feasibility Study, Design, and Implementation. Prior to the project, an Initial Investigation may be required and after the project ends, a Post Implementation Audit is required. Since it is recommended that a non-project member perform the audit, the audit is classified as maintenance versus development although the distinction is arbitrary.

A. General Description Of Project

Define who requested the project, its purpose and benefits, the scope of the project as related to the particular system, and the mandays required to complete it.

B. General Comments

1. List any major unanticipated design problems.

2. List major program problems.

3. List the changes to original design as follows:

    Description   Requested by   Additional Cost

    (You need not list all changes, but do include significant changes and totals for all changes).

4. List the scope and resources expended by the User group as an aid in the project's implementation.

5. List any comments on Implementation/Conversion (Were there significant problems? Was there a particularly successful approach?).

6. Production Comments

    a. User Forms
    b. Computer Run Time
    c. User Acceptance
    d. Miscellaneous problems: e.g., Turnaround, Test Time, Forms, Software, Turnover (input and Control, Operations)
    e. Other.

7. Overall Comments (State your general impression of the entire project).

8. Future enhancements (List any tasks that need to be accomplished to improve the implemented system).

9. Are tools available to audit the system for Data and Programming problems?

C. Project Documentation Checklist

Item	Completed
Feasibility Study	
System Narrative	
Program Narrative	
Program Listing	
System Flowchart	

Figure 8.5 Post Implementation Audit Form

D. Lines Of Code Data

This section should be included, even though all the information may not be available. If data is not available by programmer or type, it should be stated in total (by system or project).

1.   Programming language

2.

Number of		Source	Project
a.	Verbs (statements)	Compile	
b.	LOC in Proc. Div.	Compile or Libr.	
c.	Statements in Data Div.	Compile (no comments)	
d.	LOC on copylib	Copylib Count	
e.	LOC in pgm with copylib	Compile	
f.	LOC without copylib	Librarian	
g.	JCL LOC	Proclib	
h.	Comments in Proc. Div.	Calculation (b-a)	
i.	LOC generates from copylib	Calculation (e-f)	

3.   Productivity time factor (ratio of productive time to total time, generally ranges from 0.5 to 0.8)

E. Mandays

This section documents the mandays spent on the various project phases. Time reporting tasks must be defined by phase to obtain this data. Also, since time is in mandays, it should equal elapsed mandays. The following charts should be completed for each project:

1.

	Mandays		
Project Phase	DP Team	DP Mgt.	User*
Feasibility			
Design			
Implementation			
Total mandays			

*may be an estimate

Figure 8.5 (Cont.)

2.

Implementation Phase	Mandays

1.   Structured Diagrams
     Coding/Compiling
     Unit Testing	

2. S/T - Conversion	
Total	

Figure 8.5 (Cont.)

8.6 SELECTING PROJECTS FOR A PORTFOLIO

Allocation of scarce resources is the issue. How does an organization establish priorities and decide which projects are the most urgent? Sometimes the decision is based on politics; spreading DP support evenly or unevenly (whatever the case may be) among various divisions. However, this chapter does not address politics, but it does provide a detailed framework for defining corporate project benefits. Since this approach involves groups of individuals and requires resources to execute, it is not recommended for project or maintenance efforts less than 25 mandays. Also, Chapter Thirteen, (The Ultimate Mini) addresses a more general approach which complements the detail presented here.

Assume a simplified "rate of return" calculation:

$$\text{Project Payback} = \frac{\text{Development costs (\$)}}{\text{Benefits (\$)} - \text{Operations costs (\$)}}$$

There are two common mistakes associated with payback calculation: 1) no sensitivity analysis, and 2) inability to dollarize intangible benefits (intangible benefits do not directly reduce cost on corporate budgets, but may improve profits by providing more timely information to management or to the customer).

A sensitivity analysis starts by identifying the key cost/benefit factors in the payback calculation. Each of these variables is projected based on various assumptions. For example, reducing mailing volume may be a key aspect of a proposed system; assumptions on future postage increases is obviously a relevant aspect of the justification. After each variable is studied, a high and low value exist. Payback calculations are then run for the expected and worst-case situations.

Dollarizing intangible benefits is difficult but not impossible. It can be done effectively if a positive attitude exists and a framework is provided. Belief in a system is the basis of a positive attitude. The proposed steps are similar to the delphi technique of predicting, in that results are based on the experience and judgment of knowledgeable individuals.

The technique stresses cooperation among users and Data Processing personnel. The value of intangible benefits is dollarized based on experience, analogy, relative rankings, and judgment. The steps are listed below:

STEP 1   Select a group of key people who are familiar with the capability and operation of the proposed system.

STEP 2   The group should discuss and then document in detail the capabilities the system will provide so that all members have similar understanding of the project function.

STEP 3   In a "brainstorming" session, list all possible tangible and intangible benefits.

STEP 4   Research and assign a dollar value to the tangible benefits. The group should review these values so that a perspective can be maintained between tangibles and intangibles in STEP 5.

STEP 5   Addressing the first intangible benefit, each member of the group independently estimates the dollar value of the intangible benefit. The results are compared and discussed. Estimates may be modified based on the discussion. The estimating and discussion cycle is repeated one to three times. Finally, an average is recorded as the group's suggested dollar value. The estimates are more than guesses. Mentally, each individual will be comparing the benefits of previous projects to his subjective judgment of the proposed benefits and to the previously defined tangible benefits.

STEP 6   If more than one group of key individuals is involved with the project, repeat STEP 5 with each group. Then compute an overall average.

Once the benefits are established, the accepted payback calculations can be performed.

8.7 REPORTS: A BAD EXAMPLE

Situation - you are visiting a university campus for a seminar, and as a side benefit, the athletic department offers attendees a physical fitness evaluation for a nominal charge.

You take the test. You are told that comparisons are relative to others of similar age, and results will be mailed in three weeks.

The results arrive, but they appear confusing, so you compare the data with others who took the test. You conclude the report is not self-explanatory. As a matter of fact, it is difficult to deduce if a person is healthy or on the verge of collapse.

Consider Figure 8.6 which was distributed with no additional explanation. Is a high aerobic capacity encouraging? Is it encouraging to know that a 42.9 rate of recovery at the end of one minute places an individual in a 31.6 percentile? Ordinarily, personal medical history is a private matter; however, the format of this report should prevent embarrassing disclosure.

Has your staff ever produced a report which was difficult to understand? It is easy to do.

UNIVERSITY   DEPARTMENT OF HEALTH, PHYSICAL EDUCATION AND RECREATION

EXERCISE PHYSIOLOGY RESEARCH LABORATORY

PHYSICAL FITNESS EVALUATION REPORT - - - FEB 77

(GROUP COMPARISONS BASED ON DATA FROM 350MALES   AGE 18-35)
===================================
THE GROUP NOW CONSISTS OF ALL TESTS GIVEN FROM SEPT. 72 ON .

NAME JOHNSON J R		PERCENTILE	GROUP AVERAGE
		=========	=============
AGE	32.	69.8	30.1
HEIGHT (INCHES)	71.	52.0	70.9
WEIGHT--(POUNDS)	180.	57.6	175.3
PULMONARY VITAL CAPACITY* (LITERS)	5.10	59.4	4.9
*HIGHLY CORRELATED WITH BODY SIZE - ESPECIALLY HEIGHT			
BLOOD PRESSURE-SYSTOLIC**	118.	22.0	125.6
DIASTOLIC**	80.	59.0	77.9
**THERE IS A WIDE RANGE OF NORMAL FOR THESE MEASURES			
RESTING HEART RATE - (SUPINE)	62.	42.0	78.4
BICYCLE TEST WORKLOAD--(KPM/MIN)	900.		
EXERCISE HEART RATE	132.		
PREDICTED AEROBIC CAPACITY - MAX VO2 (L/MIN)	3.76	87.2	2.99
ADJUSTED FOR BODY SIZE--MAX VO2 (ML/KG/MIN)	46.0	82.1	37.90
RATE OF RECOVERY			
HEART RATE AT END OF 1ST MINUTE	102.		
PERCENT RETURN TO RESTING VALUE	42.9	31.6	52.39
HEART RATE AT END OF 2ND MINUTE	84.		
PERCENT RETURN TO RESTING VALUE	68.6	54.4	58.85

Figure 8.6 Confusing Report

PART III

CHAPTER EIGHT DISCUSSION QUESTIONS

SECTION

8.1   1.   Is developmental documentation intended for the same purpose as maintenance documentation?

8.2   2.   When will high-level "user" type languages become universally available?

8.2   3.   Is Assembler language on its way up or out?

8.3   4.   Is time reporting/simulation the panacea of project control?

8.4   5.   Can tuning really reduce computer resources by 10-15%?

8.6   6.   Why are people reluctant to estimate intangible benefits?

8.7   7.   The report example illustrates how easy it is to design worthless product. How can errors like this be prevented?

SUGGESTED READING

Mooney, John W., "Organized Program Maintenance," <u>Datamation</u>, February 1975, pp. 63-64.

PART IV

DIVISIONAL PRODUCTIVITY

"STANDARDS, STANDARDS - EVERYWHERE STANDARDS"

Anonymous

PART IV

DIVISIONAL PRODUCTIVITY

A number of management techniques are appropriate at the divisional level. The two most important, from an operational standpoint, are managing production problems and disaster recovery. The quality of standards or procedures can vary from good to poor. After discussing a bad standard and providing guidelines for a good standard, there are suggestions for organizing a standards book. Next, comments on how to improve planning productivity are presented. A potential impairment to productivity is discovered when an existing auditing standard is reviewed. The last two subjects of Chapter Nine provide advice on attending conferences and staffing training departments.

Chapter Ten violates a statement in the preface; i.e., that no theory is included. The optimal (theoretical) management training approach is proposed. However, implementation barriers prevent it from becoming a widely used, pragmatic productivity tool. The chapter offers an "ideal" management training approach which is an alternative to a week-long intensive seminar.

CHAPTER NINE

MANAGEMENT TECHNIQUES FOR THE DIVISION

Each topic in this chapter is designed to help improve productivity within the DP division. The nine management techniques are sequenced within three general categories:

I. Operational Techniques
   9.1   UCRs
   9.2   Disaster Recovery
   9.3   Bad Procedures
   9.4   Good Standards

II. Planning Techniques
   9.5   Planning Sessions
   9.6   Long-range Staff and Application Plans

III. Miscellaneous Techniques
   9.7   External Auditing
   9.8   Conferences
   9.9   Training

The comments on subjects are brief and to the point, but brevity does not imply insignificance. The reader, by comparing his or her experiences with the thoughts presented, should be able to improve management of the division.

9.1. UNUSUAL (ERROR) CONDITIONS

Assigning responsibility to unusual (error) conditions (problem abends, or terminations, software failures, etc.) is the most important tool for managing a data processing operational environment. Having a standard for communicating problems and resolutions among the DP departments is mandatory.

"Cause Code" is the key for assigning managerial responsibility. Managers are responsible for controlling unusual conditions assigned to their area. This requires a procedure to define: a document for recording unusual conditions; allowable cause codes; and a method of reporting and summarizing the results. For those without the mandatory procedure, Figure 9.1 lists one version of cause codes. It is provided to expedite the implementation.

In Chapter Seven, the value of UCRs for program problems was presented. From the attached list, note that there are seven types of cause codes (41-46, 49) which are the responsibility of the programming department (Systems Development). The impact on performance and subsequent management action varies significantly depending on the cause code. For example, assuming that a 100,000 LOC system was averaging ten code 41s (program error - no recent change) a month, the management decision may be to redesign portions of the system to assure better validation. On the other hand, if the same system were averaging ten code 43s (program error - recent change - not major installation) per month, an immediate review of change control procedures would be appropriate.

Similar examples could be listed for other cause codes, but instead, average UCR counts for major areas are listed for a DP division which executes in excess of 3 million application LOC. Remember, all errors are recorded. How does your division compare with the results in the table on the following page?

Since trends are more relevant than absolute numbers, month-by-month plots best illustrate progress (or, conversely, lack of progress).

Monthly Total	Cause Code	
26	00	UNRESOLVED
41	10	NON-HARDWARE OPERATIONAL PROBLEMS
71	11	DATA CENTER OPERATOR ERRORS
6	12	NON-HARDWARE TAPE PROBLEMS
2	20	DP ADMINISTRATIVE SERVICES
16	21	DATA ENTRY
34	22	COORDINATOR
17	23	TECHNICAL SERVICES NON-HARDWARE OPERATIONAL PROBLEMS
4	25	DATA COMMUNICATIONS GROUP
0	26	TECHNICAL SERVICES
0	29	DATA BASE ADMINISTRATION
5	30	SOFTWARE MISCELLANEOUS
7	31	SCP (INC. JES/HASP)
5	32	PROGRAM PRODUCTS AND PROPRIETARY SOFTWARE
3	33	LOCAL CODE (SOFTWARE PROGRAMMING)
72	40	SYSTEMS DEVELOPMENT
7	41	PROGRAM ERROR - NO RECENT CHANGE
14	42	PROGRAM ERROR - RECENT CHANGE - MAJOR INSTALLATION
15	43	PROGRAM ERROR - RECENT CHANGE - NOT MAJOR INSTALLATION
18	44	JCL ERROR
4	45	ERROR GENERATED AS A RESULT OF ERROR CORRECTION
6	46	STANDARDS OR PROCEDURAL VIOLATION
8	49	FAILURE IN SYSTEMS OR PARALLEL TEST BEING RUN AS PROD.
20	50	SAC OS&M SCHEDULE & MATERIAL SYSTEM
194	60	HARDWARE PROBLEMS - IBM (Terminal Probs - 18, U/R Errors - 33, Tape Errors - 74, Disk Errors - 67, Misc. Errors - 2)
31	61	HARDWARE PROBLEMS - ITEL
6	62	HARDWARE PROBLEMS - SORBUS (Includes Genesis One CRTs)
9	63	HARDWARE PROBLEMS - DATAGRAPHIX
21	69	HARDWARE PROBLEMS - OTHER VENDORS OR UNKNOWN VENDORS
6	70	REGION/SPACE MISCELLANEOUS
18	71	DASD-SPACE UNDER ALLOCATED IN JCL
1	72	DASD-SPACE NOT AVAILABLE IN PACKS
114	80	USERS
29	90	UNASSIGNED
753		Total

Figure 9.1 Unusual Condition/Report Cause Codes

9.2 DISASTER RECOVERY

The best way to avoid disaster is to install preventive measures such as physical security, dual fire extinguishing systems, partitioning of equipment, etc. But, assuming a disaster strikes, what items should be stored off-site? The answer depends on the type of the disaster. Consider the following:

1. Entire computer room and contents
2. Certain equipment
3. Data
4. Software
5. Documentation

Starting with the easiest items first, manufacturers of equipment will generally agree to priority delivery in case of an emergency. Thus, disaster recovery plan should include vendor consent for delivery in a certain time span.

Addressing off-site storage of data, software, and documentation, the only time-consuming item is defining what data files are required. For batch processing systems, the proper files and generations must be copied. A special project is required to identify all data files required for a successful pass of an application system (roughly two to three mandays effort per 100,000 LOC). Each day the appropriate files are physically stored off-site.

Online systems (vs. batch) generate special problems since communication capabilities must be duplicated or available. Remember, less than 100 percent back-up is adequate following a disaster. Loss of one day's transactions may be acceptable.

A computer room with raised flooring, adequate power, air conditioning, etc. is a more serious problem. Months would be required to construct the facilities. One recent approach to this problem is sharing space with a number of companies. The drawback is telecommunication facilities (especially if CRTs are local), but if this can be solved, sharing is probably the best approach.

During a computer disaster, a company's operation would be seriously degraded. But in justifying disaster recovery expenses, do not overlook the capacity of human ingenuity to function under adverse circumstances - without computer support.

9.3 BAD STANDARDS/PROCEDURES

It is easier to write a bad standard/procedure than it is to write an effective one.

Having a 400 page standards book is not necessarily commendable. Since poorly written or unnecessary standards create bureaucracy, standards should be written only when they are judged the appropriate technique for resolving problems. It is easy to develop standard-mania. To avoid this mania, each proposed standard should be subject to the following criteria:

1. Does it provide necessary control?

2. Is it enforceable; i.e., are violations detected as a natural course of reviews or exception reports?

3. For individuals to accomplish their jobs, is the information necessary (an opinion or suggestion is not a standard)?

4. Is the standard an effective method of accomplishing the objective?

5. Will the standard be referenced?

If a proposed standard does not receive an affirmative response for all the above, throw it out. In most corporations, 10 - 20 percent of the standards would be eliminated by the above criteria. Note the example on the following page. Does it pass? You decide.

The Training Project Leader will insure that the following procedure is followed.

Person Requesting Equipment:

1. Contacts member of DP Technical Services Training Staff.

2. Provides information about the type of equipment and the date and time it is needed.

Member of DP Technical Services Training Staff:

3. Checks "Desk Master Diary" labeled "Reservation of D.P.T.S. Equipment" in the DP Training Library to see if the equipment is available on the date requested.

4. Responds in one of two ways:

    a. Equipment available:

        1) Informs person who is requesting the equipment that it is available on the date needed.

        2) Enters the following information in the Desk Master Diary under the appropriate date:

            a) Name of person reserving equipment.

            b) Time period that the equipment will be used.

            c) Type of equipment being reserved.

            d) Serial number of equipment when there is more than one of the same type (e.g., audio cassette players).

    b. Equipment unavailable:

        1) Informs person requesting equipment that it is not available.

        2) Suggests other possible sources for equipment.

Figure 9.2 Standard for Reserving Education Equipment

9.4 "GOOD" STANDARDS

Seventy-five percent of DP standards apply to the Life Cycle of a system. The majority of these require interdepartment concurrence and development. So why not organize the standards similar to the life cycle evolution (feasibility, design, implementation, and maintenance)?

Generally, the organization would be as follows:

1.0   Life Cycle (75% of standards)
       Feasibility
       Design
       Implementation
       Maintenance

2.0   Software

3.0   Operations

4.0   Data Input

5.0   Data Base

6.0   Training

7.0   Software Packages

8.0   Management

All sections, except the first, apply only to the specific department. A more detailed outline follows on the next two pages.

1.0   Life Cycle Standards

1.100   Definition of Life Cycle
1.200   Project Phase Plans

1.300   Initial Investigation Phase
            1.310   Submitting DP Services Requests
            1.320   Checklist of Project Activities

1.400   Feasibility Study Phase
            1.410   Guidelines for Writing
            1.420   Project Estimating
            1.430   Manday Definition
            1.440   Costing Standard
            1.450   Review Meetings

1.500   Design Phase - Batch Systems
            1.510   System Documentation
            1.520   Naming Conventions
            1.530   Program Estimating
            1.540   Security
            1.550   Review Meetings

1.600   Design Phase - Online Systems
            1.610   System Documentation
            1.620   Naming Conventions
            1.630   Program Estimating
            1.640   Security Controls
            1.650   Data Base Conventions
            1.660   Review Meetings

1.700   Implementation - Batch Systems
            1.710   JCL Standards
            1.720   Testing Standards
            1.730   Turnover (Operations) Documentation
            1.740   Reviews

1.800   Implementation - Online Systems
            1.810   Standard Work Units
            1.820   Testing Standards
            1.830   Documentation
            1.840   Security Reviews

1.900   Post Implementation
            1.910   Post Audit
            1.920   UCR
            1.930   Modifying Production Systems
            1.940   One Time Production

Figure 9.3 Organization of Standards

2.0   Software

    2.100   Generating Operating Systems
    2.200   Applying PTFs
    2.300   Applying Local Modifications
    2.400   CICS Library Update
    2.500   Installing Software Packages

3.0   Operations

    3.100   Job Descriptions
    3.200   Training Operators
    3.300   Production Processing
    3.400   One-Time Production
    3.500   Report Distribution
    3.600   Start-up Procedure
    3.700   Scheduling Guidelines

4.0   Data Input

    4.100   Training Operators
    4.200   Machine Operation
    4.300   Logging Procedure

5.0   Data Base

    5.100   Dictionary Maintenance
    5.200   Data Base Conversion

6.0   Training

    6.100   Courses Offered
    6.200   Training Cycle

7.0   Software Packages

    7.100   Date Routines
    7.200   Utilities
    7.300   Microfilm
    7.400   TSO

8.0   Management

    8.100   User Facilities
    8.200   Disaster Recovery
    8.300   Performance Measures

Figure 9.3 (Cont.)

9.5 PLANNING SESSIONS

IBM supports and endorses the concept of a planning session for short-term, intermediate, and long-term planning. Preparation for the session is as follows:

Reserve two to three mandays for the appropriate managers and to avoid interruptions, meet outside normal working environment. Mechanics of the session involve a series of five steps:

1. State objectives (which coincide with corporate objectives)

2. Define problems

3. List possible solutions to problems

4. Define to-do's (tasks which bring about a solution)

5. Assign responsibility and completion dates.

For each step, comments or results are documented on large papers and posted in the room so all participants can easily read them. A secretary later types from the papers. There are two unwritten rules which apply to the planning session: if other members criticize the spelling or writing of some member of the group documenting the results, then that person becomes the scribe; also, if any member thinks the conversation is proceeding off the subject, he says loudly "baloney," or some such word to get the meeting back on track.

Planning sessions can be an effective management tool; however, there are potential problems. First, a priority step might not be included; i.e., minor problems are treated the same as major problems. This may result in expending manpower resources unnecessarily. IBM may have intentionally forgotten this step because solutions resulting in hardware, software, or training support generate revenue - and why not budget for everything?

Second, it is very easy to mix short-range immediate problems with longer range problems. This can result in a staff meeting atmosphere which is not the purpose of an intermediate or long-range planning session. Thus, decide on the type of session and stick to it.

Third, IBM personnel generally participate in and may conduct the planning sessions. For the first session and for other long-range issues, their input is recommended. But for short-range planning, which mainly involves interface among department managers, less value is derived from their presence. After all, IBM's objectives are not always your objectives.

By all means, planning sessions are recommended, but keep the objectives of the meeting clear, and prioritize the solutions.

9.6 LONG RANGE STAFF AND APPLICATION PLANNING

Everyone talks about long-range application and staff planning, but unfortunately, the key input to a good plan is knowledge of the future, which is not always available. Nonetheless, a format and technique for planning is the first step. The method presented is for application planning versus hardware planning. The steps below are linked to figures 9.4 and 9.5.

STEP 1   In a brainstorming session, identify all potential developmental projects. Input from user divisions is essential, although it may be indirect vs. direct. A written description of the project is required.

STEP 2   Scope the potential projects in manyears of effort.

STEP 3   Prioritize the potential projects.

STEP 4   List the existing staffing level for support and development in a budget entity.

STEP 5   Plan projects three to five years into the future, and reflect staffing levels. Projects which are implemented during this time frame increase the support level.

The result of these five steps is a long-range plan, which is of interest to other DP division personnel and user divisions. Acknowledging that actual staffing levels and decisions on project initiation are related to corporate profitability, the plan is still a valuable tool.

(Step 1) Description	(Step 2) Man Years	(Step 3) Priority	(Step 5) Year
A. Everyday			
1. Auto-Upgrade	1	Committed	80
2. Dealer Systems	1	High	80
3. Online Access to Information	1	Medium	80
4. Promotion Hold File	1-4	Medium-Low	82
5. Delivery Systems	1/2	Medium-Low	80
6. ED Product Data Base	5-10	Low	83+
B. Billing			
1. Invoice Redesign	3	High	80
2. Support Liberty	1/2	Committed	80
3. S-200	1	Medium-Low	?
4. Support Distribution Center	1	Committed	80
C. Name & Address			
1. Customer Data Base	3	Low	82

Figure 9.4 Summary of Potential Projects

LONG-RANGE PLANNING

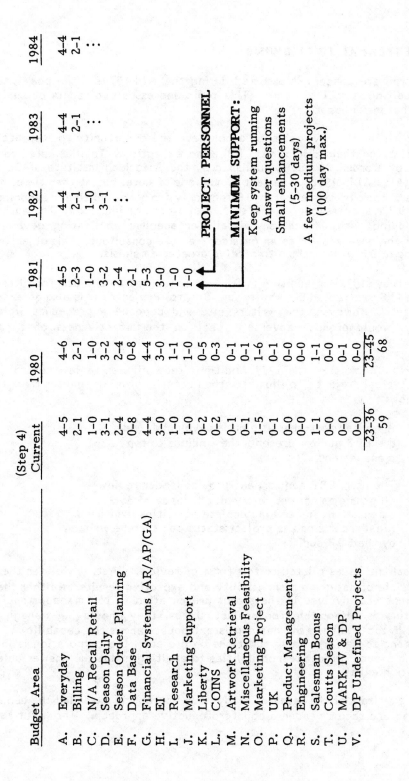

Budget Area	(Step 4) Current	1980	1981	1982	1983	1984
A. Everyday	4-5	4-6	4-5	4-4	4-4	4-4
B. Billing	2-1	2-1	2-3	2-1	2-1	2-1
C. N/A Recall Retail	1-0	1-0	1-0	1-0		
D. Season Daily	3-1	3-2	3-2	3-1		
E. Season Order Planning	2-4	2-4	2-4	...	...	...
F. Data Base	0-8	0-8	2-1			
G. Financial Systems (AR/AP/GA)	4-4	4-4	5-3			
H. EI	3-0	3-0	3-0			
I. Research	1-0	1-1	1-0			
J. Marketing Support	1-0	1-0	1-0			
K. Liberty	0-2	0-5				
L. COINS	0-2	0-3				
M. Artwork Retrieval	0-1	0-1				
N. Miscellaneous Feasibility	0-1	0-1				
O. Marketing Project	1-5	1-6				
P. UK	0-1	0-1				
Q. Product Management	0-0	0-0				
R. Engineering	0-0	0-0				
S. Salesman Bonus	1-1	1-1				
T. Coutts Season	0-0	0-0				
U. MARK IV & DP	0-0	0-1				
V. DP Undefined Projects	0-0	0-0				
	23-36	23-45				
	59	68				

PROJECT PERSONNEL

MINIMUM SUPPORT:

Keep system running
Answer questions
Small enhancements
 (5-30 days)
A few medium projects
 (100 day max.)

Step 5

Figure 9.5 Long Range Planning

-112-

9.7 AUDITING, EXTERNAL TO DP DIVISION

Auditing, as a corporate concern, blossomed during the mid-1970s. The peak year for interest in DP auditing is still to come. This topic addresses two facets of auditing - objectivity and a potential hazard.

Those working in a specific environment do not have the opportunity to step back and reflect without bias, on their discipline. DP is no exception. To illustrate, consider Auditing & EDP, by Gordon B. Davis, published by the American Institute of Certified Public Accounts (AICPA) in 1968. The text is now out of date, but at that time, it may have been the best book in existence on DP, not only from an auditing standpoint, but also as a text for DP managers (operations, software, programming, etc.). The author did not mire his thinking with unnecessary details or specific application development problems. Rather, he observed DP as an outsider - a pure consultant. This objectivity is the reason auditing in DP will continue to receive greater emphasis.

The most recent study (1977) on auditing in DP was conducted by the Stanford Research Institute and titled "Systems Audit - Ability and Control Project." It is also an excellent objective document. However, the writers cite and condone a procedure which, if followed literally, would produce adverse impact on the effectiveness of a project development team.

In Part III (General Controls) of the 1977 Auditing Study, fifteen review control points are defined for a typical project. To illustrate the potential problem, quotes from two of these reviews follow:

> A revised cost-benefit plan is developed, and
> the EDP auditor presents the findings to top
> management.

> The user, EDP auditor, and project leader review
> all problems not yet resolved, adequacy of doc-
> umentation, and any incomplete activities identified.
> Final reports on the project status can then be written
> by the EDP auditor.

There are a few salient issues related to this form of review. First, it violates the basic management principle of assigning responsibility and expecting results. Neither the user nor DP management are involved in the status presentation to top management - how absurd! If auditing is responsible for project status, they should be managing the project. Second, if top management has consistent doubts about the capability of users and DP management to perform their functions on projects, the corporation is in deep trouble. Assigning pseudo project responsibilities to auditing is not the answer unless an exceptional condition exists.

To summarize, the writers of the research study have improperly extended the beneficial aspects of auditing and recommended a counterproductive approach. Watch out for this potential hazard.

9.8 COMPUTER EXHIBITIONS/CONFERENCES

Many excellent conferences are sponsored throughout the year. Some major exhibitions include the following:

> NCC (National Computer Conference)
> INFO
> EXPO
> INTERFACE
> IFIP

Two suggestions are submitted to conference attendees: 1) Have a specific purpose, and 2) Write a trip report.

1. Having 300-plus companies (at the larger conferences) compete for the attention of 35,000 individuals produces an overwhelming impact on the visitor. It is impossible to obtain meaningful information in all areas. Thus, assuming an individual is attending a conference for more than general education, the only way to assure a productive trip is to have specific interests defined in advance. For example, evaluating intelligent terminal capabilities and costs is a specific objective which could be accomplished in two to three days.

2. Trip reports should be written in memo form, and made detailed enough to convey the success of the mission.

    A trip report should contain the following basic information:

    1. Date, duration, expense, location, those attending

    2. Purpose of the trip

    3. Completion of trip objectives

    4. Quality of instruction or presentation

    5. General comments, evaluation, and recommendations.

    The format is flexible and should be modified when applicable.

9.9 TRAINING, PERSONNEL STAGNATION

Training implies classes and instruction, right? Not necessarily. Consider the following definition of training:

> Planning individual assignments which enhance technical and personnel development, and providing the necessary direction to accomplish the assignments.

The two distinct aspects of training are classroom and on-the-job. Classroom training connotes the ability to perform skillfully, which implies skillful use of the basic tools. How does one become an expert at structure programming, Warnier diagrams, or top-down design techniques? The answer is, of course, by using the concepts to solve real problems. And this fact is the reason training departments stagnate. Training personnel continue to work with well-defined classroom samples, and their skill level consequently remains at the basic level.

The only way to assure a dynamic, competent training organization is to enforce a two-year maximum tenure for instructors. After two years, "back to the real world."

PART IV

CHAPTER NINE DISCUSSION QUESTIONS

SECTION

9.1   1.   Why is it mandatory to document the cause of unusual conditions?

9.1   2.   How many UCRs would you expect when installing a ten-manyear project?

9.2   3.   Why is disaster recovery important to a corporation?   Does hardware reliability decrease this importance?

9.3   4.   Why are poor standards written?

9.5   5.   Why are planning sessions important?

9.7   6.   Should auditors have project responsibility?

9.8   7.   Why are major computer exhibitions overwhelming?

BIBLIOGRAPHY

Davis, Gordon B., Auditing & EDP, The American Institute of Certified Public Accountants, Inc., 1968.

Stanford Study, ''Systems Audit and Control Project,'' 1977.

Perry, William E. and Fitzgerald, Jerry, ''Designing for Auditability,'' Datamation, Aug. 1977, pp. 46-50.

CHAPTER TEN

A PHILOSOPHY FOR MANAGEMENT TRAINING

To introduce Chapter Ten, excerpts from the editor's readout (John Kirkley, <u>Datamation</u>, July 1978) appear below:

> At an NCC cocktail party last month, we ran into our old friend, Dr. Persiflage Melon, noted management consultant and small-arms expert. He wanted to talk to us about a recent editorial where we commented that one of the DP professional's toughest jobs was being a manager.

> "Nonsense," said Melon, sipping a martini. "Managing is the simplest thing in the world as long as you remember that there are no rules and no one knows what he's doing anyway."

> "But look what happens. A manager begins foundering and so he packs himself off to an AMA seminar or some such rot. There, a middleaged man with a crew cut and short-sleeved shirt loads him up with the Hawthorne Effect, Maslow's hierarchy of needs, and other folklore straight out of the fifties. He worked through a gaggle of case studies with his fellow neophytes and, at the end of a week, returns to work with a three-ring binder full of useless information, ready to terrorize his employees. The result is chaos."

> But what's a manager to do? we asked.

> "Simplicity itself," said Melon. "Successful management is the application of three basic ingredients: first, adopting a management style; second, making decisions, and third, managing time - your own and that of your employees."

> "Now, as to adopting a management style, my advice is simple - don't. Nothing is more ludicrous than a pussycat trying to behave like a panzer tank commander. Or a grade-A, dyed-in-the-wool s.o.b. trying to be Mr. Nice-Guy. So be yourself, be honest. You won't fool anybody for long anyway."

> Well, what about decision making?, we asked, Risk analysis, decision tables, and all that?

> "Nothing to it," said Melon, helping himself to another martini. "You gather as much information as you can reasonably gather, sleep on it, and the next day make a decision. If you make the wrong decision, you make another. If you make too many wrong decisions, you shouldn't be in that line of work anyway."

Seems straightforward enough, we said, But what about
time management?

"Ah, one of my favorite subjects," said Melon, waving his
arms expansively and spilling gin on a passing advertising
salesman..."By using a few simple ideas - goal setting,
working on the most important things first - you'll soon
have your time under control. From there it's a simple
matter to help your employees organize their time
successfully."

And that's all there is to managing?, we asked. You make
hundreds of thousands of dollars each year from the major
corporations as a management consultant. And that's all
you tell them?

"Good heavens, no," said Melon aghast. "They'd never stand
for it. No, what I do is gather them together in a room for
a week's intensive seminar. I give them a three-ring binder,
tell them all about Maslow, Herzberg and McGregor, and show
them Peter Drucker films. They love it."

Melon, we said, we're beginning to suspect you're a bit of
a fraud.

"Alas," said Melon, delicately fishing the olive out of his
martini, "it does appear that way, doesn't it?"

The value of any management training program is measured by whether or not a positive
improvement in management results. If a man attends a class or seminar and does not
take anything permanent from the experience, it has been of no value.

Thus, a philosophy of management training is proposed which takes advantage of existing
experiences, acknowledges the thoughts of other professional people, provides an
opportunity for self-development, capitalizes on the benefits of a seminar, and integrates
the management philosophy into the environment of the individual.

After managing for a few years, each manager develops his own individual management
philosophy. It may not be written down, and it may not consciously be related to other
philosophies, but it does exist. A management philosophy is not a theoretical concept - it
is a manager executing the planning, organizing, motivating, and controlling functions
within his scope of responsibility.

The proposed philosophy of management training expedites the learning process of a
manager by: 1) utilizing available management experiences, 2) exposing the manager to
the thoughts of other professionals, 3) integrating self-development into the process, and
4) relating management concepts to an individual's organizational environment.

This chapter proposes an alternative to typical management training approaches. The
philosophy of management training presented is a four step process based on the

following assumptions:

1. Resources for management training are available within an organization.

2. Superior management philosophies exist.

3. Effective management training originates through self-development.

4. Learning must be applied or executed within an organization.

STEP 1 ESTABLISH COMMITMENT

A commitment on the part of the responsible manager to the concept of internal, self-development management training is the first step.

Today, the commonly accepted approach to management training involves a classroom type environment where the concept of planning, organizing, motivating, and controlling are elaborated.

The hypothetical company XYZ, one of the world's main suppliers of widgets, will provide us a source for various case studies. Within this framework, merits of various organizational charts are reviewed, job descriptions analyzed, and the concept of management by objectives is presented. The class members generally participate in group activities in order to demonstrate the central points.

Since this type of management training is an expensive proposition ($500-$1,500/week), one might ask the benefits of the training. For new or potential managers, the basic concepts may provide a framework for an individual management philosophy. For the older manager, the major benefit is the confidence derived from discussing concepts already experienced.

These benefits are of value, but the real question is, "Will the manager improve his performance as a result of this class?" Ask yourself what specifically was retained from your last management seminar. Perhaps a person could list two or three substantial changes in his behavior, but this is generally not the case. Management training is not a one-time classroom activity.

We can conclude, then, that deficiencies exist in the typical management training approach. The two main weaknesses are not capitalizing on self-development and not relating the concepts to the manager's specific organizational environment.

The basis of the management training is the experiences and thoughts of the existing management team within an organization. The combined experience of this group assuredly exceeds fifteen to twenty years. This source of learning is the best basis for effective management development.

The proposed philosophy requires that the responsible manager form an action plan which involves the manager and his subordinates. The first step is to discuss the concept with the management team and become committed to the concept.

STEP 2 SELECT MATERIAL

Capitalizing on the thoughts of others is the intent of Step 2. Management philosophies have been documented by a number of great thinkers. The subject is related to human nature and consequently does not change dramatically over the years. For example, the world may wait a long time before Drucker's thoughts are expressed more eloquently.

Step 2, therefore, consists of selecting sources of material from one of the outstanding management-related books. The selection process should be in the form of group participation. If individuals on the management team have a preference for a given book or author, that is a good reason for selecting the text. Also, it is better to thoroughly read and comprehend one or two authors than it is to just browse multiple authors. Also, copies of the books should be purchased - if they are worth reading they are worth referencing.

Various texts address different aspects of general management. Two books which address the manager's position are Up the Organization by Robert Townsend (Alfred A. Knopf, Inc., 1970) and The Effective Executive by Peter Drucker (Harper and Row, 1966).

STEP 3 PROMOTE SELF-DEVELOPMENT

Step 3 is based on the premise that technical training is not analogous to management training. Formal education satisfies the former but not the latter.

In the environment of a business manager, learning is a self-development process. Development is defined as behavior change based on learning experiences. Self implies that the motivation for learning originates in an individual.

Does anyone remember anything other than the terms Theory X and Theory Y from college classes? Management actions and decisions are based on a personal philosophy. It is important to become cognizant of this philosophy so it can grow and develop.

Step 3 sets the stage for self-development, by demanding that an individual relate his thoughts to established thinkers. Each person must document why the ideas/philosophies studied are good or bad.

One method to accomplish this thought process is to rate each chapter on a 0-5 scale. The numbers have the following definitions:

5	Exceptional value
4	Very valuable
3	Valuable
2	Some value
1	Worthless
0	Thoroughly disagreeable

The chapters can then be discussed one at a time. In addition, each member of the management team should prioritize the five most relevant concepts an author presents. This list is also input to the seminar discussion of Step 4.

The problems managers face will be reflected in the prioritized list of concepts. Thus, an excellent means of relating management principles to real decisions is provided.

In summary, consciously relating one's thoughts to those of other professionals is the key to permanent changes in behavior. Self-motivation is facilitated, since individuals have the opportunity to expand on their own ideas.

STEP 4 STRUCTURE OF A SEMINAR

In isolation, a man can form an acceptable management philosophy. Using a seminar approach as Step 4 indicates, the results will assuredly be better. Exchanging ideas with peers who face similar problems is a well-known technique.

A manager's philosophy is influenced by the organization and its environment. Thus, effective development must integrate formal practices into an environment. Accomplishing this process is the intent of Step 4.

The seminar should be structured such that all participate. One technique is for each person to list the five most important aspects of the book. Then, going around the room, each person explains the next item on his list which has not been discussed. After a composite list is completed, an attempt to prioritize the concepts is essential. Dialogue over the ranking of the concepts is an integral part of the process.

The topics and discussion will integrate managers' experiences with immediate problems. For example, if bureaucracy is an issue, ways of reducing red tape in the organization may be discussed.

The management functions must be related to a specific organization before action results. In other words, 1) Is the existing planning structure adequate at the current time? 2) Are positions in the organization designed to motivate the type of individuals filling the position? 3) Is resource allocation shifting, based on external factors; and if so, is there awareness of the potential impact? These types of questions are inevitable when a team of managers discusses management.

This approach will produce beneficial, permanent results in a specific organization. It addresses real world problems encountered when executing the management functions.

WISHFUL THINKING?

Even though 95 percent of all managers will endorse the concepts presented in this chapter, the philosophy will not be widely accepted. Can you explain why?

WHY "A PHILOSOPHY OF MANAGEMENT TRAINING" WILL NOT BE WIDELY IMPLEMENTED

The key individual responsible for implementation is the boss. He is the one who budgets the time, conducts the seminar, provides leadership, and explains how management principles are applied within the framework of the corporation.

He is also the reason the philosophy becomes an academic concept versus a pragmatic concept. The boss is human, and like all humans, his decisions are not based 100 percent on facts or text book management principles. He makes decisions based on intuition, emotion, preferences, politics, etc. Thus, implementing the philosophy creates vulnerability for the manager. His thought process is exposed. Consequently, it is difficult to maintain "distance" between himself and those reporting to him.

The philosophy is endorsed by 95 percent of management, but very few managers will train others according to this philosophy. Thus, the one-week intensive management seminar will continue as the acceptable method of educating managers.

PART IV

CHAPTER TEN DISCUSSION QUESTIONS

1. Is it desirable to receive basic training on-the-job?

2. In the year 2000, will managers conduct training seminars for those who report to them?

SUGGESTED READING

Drucker, Peter F., <u>Management, Tasks, Responsibilities, Practices</u>, Harper & Row, 1973.

BIBLIOGRAPHY

Townsend, Robert, <u>Up the Organization</u>, Alfred A. Knopf, Inc., 1970.

Drucker, Peter F., <u>The Effective Executive</u>, Harper & Row, 1966.

Kirkley, John, "Editors Readout," <u>Datamation</u>, July 1978, p. 87.

PART V

CORPORATE PRODUCTIVITY

"THERE ARE AS MANY USES FOR COMPUTERS AS

THERE ARE FOR ELECTRICITY"

Anonymous

PART V

CORPORATE PRODUCTIVITY

Effective company utilization of DP is addressed through three topics: Data Base, Distributed Processing, and Organizational Issues.

The benefits of Data Base may not be an all-encompassing MIS, but Data Base does have substantial benefits to the DP organization. Will Data Base ultimately increase productivity, or is there any truth in the following?

> Ironically, after ten years, when the DP community
> has finally learned to use existing technology
> efficiently, it will be starting over with more
> complex tools in an unending search for DP utopia.

Chapter Eleven (Data Base) does not attempt to "disprove" the benefits of Data Base; but rather, to present the other side of the story, providing realism to the subject. If it results in realistic expectations for Data Base by top management, then it will have accomplished its objective.

Chapter Twelve (Distributed Processing) describes how applications are implemented on hardware. Definitions of distributed and decentralized systems aid the discussion. However, the most effective way of definition is definition by example within a corporation. Why use abstract terminology when real world examples exist? Next, the discussion on Distributed Processing attempts to segregate communication factors from the business decision. Can ten minicomputers outperform a 158 (an IBM 370/158) at one-half the cost? Are minicomputers popular because of the continuing failure of big CPUs to provide reliable service?

Chapter Thirteen (The Ultimate Mini) raises a few basic observations about the benefits of DP in a corporation. The chapter addresses productivity in the corporate environment, classifies computer applications by type, relates applications to productivity, and warns top management about exploding DP people-costs outside of DP.

Chapter Fourteen (Productivity and the Organization) relates various organizational structures to corporate productivity. As the functions performed in DP during the 1950-60 era emerged in user organizations, what has happened to productivity? Section One explains the forces which have and will influence organization changes relating to DP, based on organizational structure. Section Two discusses barriers to productivity in the DP and user organizations during the 1975-85 and 1985-95 time periods. By understanding these barriers, management will be able to operate more effectively.

CHAPTER ELEVEN

DATA BASE - UTOPIA OR BOONDOGGLE?

The concept of Data Base has permeated the corporate world. Executives speak in terms of controlling corporate data and integrating systems to provide more timely information. Dick Nolan, Managing the Crisis in Data Processing, pp. 115-126, projected significant increases for the corporate Data Processing budget as a corporation evolves. Assimilating Data Base technology results in a fifth and sixth stage of growth and additional expense. In general, Data Processing has been revitalized by Data Base - everything good which can be accomplished is placed under the "umbrella" of Data Base.

But what does it all mean? Has the same tune been played before: will Data Base fulfill the expectations of top management, or will disappointment result? The following statements were extracted from various publications. Obviously, there is conflict between the two columns, Utopia and Boondoggle.

UTOPIA	BOONDOGGLE
Data Base Approach	
"It facilitates the sharing of data, and provides better and more timely information to management."	"Nothing more than technical jargon, misapplied in most cases to perfectly ordinary traditional applications."
Data as a Corporate Resource	
"The normal management tools of budget, appropriation and other controls can be brought to bear."	"Users think of the data associated with their application as their personal data. You just don't appoint a Data Base Administrator and eliminate those feelings."
Cost Justification	
"Investments in hardware, software and personnel must be based on the needs of the Data Base control system, not on the requirements for specific applications."	"Each system or sub-system should be evaluated on its own merits; only if justified in terms of cost reduction or profit improvement would it be designed and implemented."
Data Base/MIS	
"Collection of data logically organized to meet the information and time requirements of an entire organization (or division)."	"After 7 years of evolving an MIS to meet some of these needs, we have abandoned any near-term goals for the complete MIS envisioned by the management science fiction writers during the late 1960s. None exists in any company now."

Before presenting the definitions which are required for a logical discourse, it is interesting to speculate on the motivation of Data Base beneficiaries.

WHO IS CONTRIBUTING TO THE CONFUSION?

An individual's perspective can induce positive or negative acceptance of Data Base: consider the four positions of Computer Marketing Representative, Corporate Executive, Data Base Administrator, and Development Manager (responsible for designing, implementing, and maintaining Data Processing Application Systems).

Since Data Base does require additional hardware, the position of a Marketing Representative requires no explanation. The Corporate Executive maintains mild optimism for a management information system (MIS). Enough credibility exists, and the potential payback is so high (competitive edge) that additional budget dollars may be insignificant. For self-preservation, the Data Base Administrator has joined forces with the Marketing Representative. It is interesting to note that literature surveys on Data Base implementation have yet to publish a failure. But since Data Base personnel are the respondents, this might be expected - something like a fox guarding the hen-house.

Occasionally, and only occasionally, individuals who have been developing systems attempt to clarify the vague term, Data Base. For example, all of the comments in the second column on the previous list of statements were quoted from previous or current Development Managers or Analysts.

Is it possible that a conspiracy has been formed by those benefitting from the all-encompassing term, Data Base? Well, that might be going too far. Especially since the bias of the Development Manager (resistance to change or loss of control, etc.) has been ignored. Enough generalities, the precedent for rational discussions starts with definitions.

DEFINITIONS

1. Data Field - one or more characters which has a defined meaning, e.g., account number, name, address, units sold during week, etc.

2. Data - one or more data fields which have meaning together, e.g., name and address.

3. Information - data organized in a useful manner (the terms data and information are used interchangeably), e.g., alphabetical telephone book.

4. Query Language - high-level (easily learned) language which facilitates extracting and summarizing data or information. A query language provides the ability to convert data or information into more useful forms, e.g., phone book sorted in number sequence.

5. Online Access - interactive, timely (seconds), visual (CRT, printer, etc.) access to data or information.

6. Data Base Access Method - a tool for reading and writing data. It replaces the typical sequential or index sequential access routines and allows traditional flexibility in technical design.

7. Management Information System (MIS) -

   a) A system which supplies information for "operating" decisions. May be an application system (see 9). Would address questions like, "which accounts ordered over 1,000 units of product X Y Z?"

   b) A system which supplies information for top "executive" level decisions, e.g., "Evaluate an increase in the advertising budget in light of the company's pricing strategy and distribution channels."

8. Data Base Management System (DBMS) - the software package which supports a Data Base Access Method, a dictionary, physical and logical data bases, communication facilities, and data manipulation features, e.g., IMS/VS, TOTAL, ADABAS, System 2000, IDMS and DATACOM/DB.

9. Data Processing Application System - an integrated group of procedures, hardware, and software that serves one central business function. Can be referred to as "operating" MIS, e.g., Payroll, Sales Reporting, Manufacturing, Scheduling, Materials Requirements Planning (MRP).

10. Data Base -

   a) Collection of data either physically or logically related. Used synonymously with file or data set. A Data Base Access Method is required for logical relationships.

   b) General term which encompasses all of the above.

This last definition (10.b) is the source of much confusion. The "umbrella" of Data Base applies to all aspects of Data Processing. Thus, the central thrust of this section is to clarify what is independent of Data Base and what is not. Since Data Base is an expensive proposition, executives should understand what they are buying.

WHAT IF DATA BASE DID NOT EXIST?

For a moment, assume the Data Processing Industry had not discovered DBMS, and thus, traditional Data Processing techniques were still in vogue. What would be the direction of the Data Processing industry? The concentration would be in the following areas:

   1. MIS
   2. Online access to information
   3. High-level query languages
   4. Productivity
   5. Data dictionary
   6. Design reviews

MIS: THE NATURE OF THE PROBLEM

For twenty years, system designers have struggled with the concept of MIS. There have been some successes for application systems in operating areas (definition 7.a). However, MIS has the connotation of an executive-oriented system (definition 7.b). Implementing an executive MIS was basically abandoned by corporations until Data Base became popular. Now, executive MIS is viewed as synonymous with Data Base. Does the technology of DBMS eradicate previous constraints?

The theory of MIS is based on the premise that complex data relationships are necessary among various applications: allowing designers to link common data is the function of a DBMS, and consequently, the reason for MIS success. The fallacy in this logic is that technology is not the limitation. Traditional techniques of validation, sorting, and updating data have allowed common data among systems for years. However, there are two pragmatic problems that reduce the probability of MIS: conflicting objectives and ownership of data.

Consider the typical Data Processing applications serving a corporation (MIS as in 7.a):

1. Engineering
2. Master Scheduling
3. Forecasting
4. Order Processing
5. Material Requirements Planning (MRP)
6. Manufacturing
7. Inventory Control/Distribution
8. Sales Reporting
9. Accounting/Financial
10. Employee Information/Payroll

The one area where a generalized DBMS has proven itself is in Materials Requirement Planning (MRP). This is the classic application for Data Base Access Methods.

In designing an application system, the designers list the specific function to be included, define inputs, define outputs, and determine the processing logic. The single objective of the design is to assist operational individuals (i.e., engineers, accountants, salesmen, etc.) in executing at the operational (versus executive) level. Even with the single objective of satisfying one group of individuals within one application, many Data Processing projects fail. Now add two more objectives (satisfy top management's information needs and resolve interrelations with other systems) and the complexity of the project more than doubles. The limitations are based on conflicting objectives, project complexity and human capabilities. In case this sounds pessimistic, consider that no company has implemented a fully integrated system to date.

An analogous situation exists for the designers of combat aircraft. One plane cannot suit multiple roles (fighter, attack craft, interceptor, and bomber); but rather, a plane is built to accomplish one specific function.

The second inherent problem associated with MIS is ownership of data. In each of the application areas, interpretation and use of data has evolved over the years. Management in the application area control the data and are responsible for its timeliness and accuracy. Sharing application data is conceptually a sound idea, but what happens when the materials manager is asked to change his definition of "material on hand" to coincide with the accounting manager's definition? Further, assume that the accounting department needs require a month-end cut-off date, but the field, as used in the materials department, is updated depending on the work load of purchase orders to be processed in the materials department. Should materials change the priority of work, so accounting can be happy with an exact cut-off time?

At this point, the Data Base Administrator theoretically takes charge and resolves the issue. Well, maybe, but there hasn't been much success. Implementing common definitions sounds feasible, but ownership of data is so strong that the concept is difficult to implement.

OTHER BENEFITS?

Benefits for online access to information, query languages, productivity, data dictionary, and design reviews are consistently stated as direct benefits of Data Base. Actually, online access to information is independent of Data Base. True, DBMS generally support online access, but online access is also part of every large computer manufacturer's standard support package.

The benefits of query languages, easy to use extract languages, such as GIS (IBM) or MARK IV (Informatics) is also independent of Data Base. Vendors of query languages claim that any standard file can be read.

Productivity within the Data Processing environment is a function of structured design/programming, quality control, system test, project management, and team organization. Refining each of these techniques has benefitted Data Processing, and possibly improved productivity 10-25%. Is it possible that a DBMS will match this productivity increase on design and programming tasks? Or is the effort simply shifted to a separate group of individuals working in the Data Base organization? To the author's knowledge, no study has quantitatively demonstrated a productivity increase for the total design and programming effort.

In a typical, large organization, a major application system may contain 100 programs and include 300-1,000 data fields. A data dictionary defines each field and links these fields to files and programs. Automating this function assures consistent documentation and provides standardization within Data Processing.

Establishing an independent Data Base group and requiring design reviews with the development personnel is also an important and desirable function. All too often, designers tend to reinvent the wheel. Data Base can assure a second option on integral design features such as file definition, processing logic, system flow, etc.

However, the point is that progress in each of these areas would continue to proceed independently even if Data Base had not become a popular topic.

DATA AS A CORPORATE ASSET

The assets of the corporation are men, machines, materials, money, and data. IBM has stated that data is an asset and, in a way, it is. Information is required in every aspect of the organization's operation. Of course, its value is dependent on'how people use the information in decision making. But data can be said to have an intrinsic worth similar to other assets. Thus, as with men, machines, materials, and money, controlling the accuracy and security of data are comprehensible concepts. Is a Data Base the only means of controlling data, and is data currently controlled?

Yes, data is accurate in organizations today. It is maintained accurately at the operational level. In most instances, data is self-correcting. For example, if an individual receives a paycheck with the name spelled incorrectly, the person will take action to correct the data. Also, assume a nonexistent part number is ordered; how long before the purchase manager is notified and rectifies the problem?

Since data is serving an operational purpose, the users have a vested interest in its accuracy for each application. This does not imply consistency among application systems. There are inconsistencies, and if operating problems result, a manual or Data

Processing solution is possible. In other words, redundant data exists, but within the application area, the data is maintained as accurately as demanded.

Just as the security of money is important, so too is the security of data. Information requiring security may involve any of the following functional areas:

> Payroll
> Accounts Receivable
> Accounts Payable
> Engineering Specifications
> Cost Accounting
> New Product Development

In existing organizations, manual and automated security measures are in effect. If security becomes a problem, appropriate action is initiated. The auditing staff has the ultimate responsibility for assuring the security measures.

Thus, it is concluded that data is analogous to other assets; but, contrary to popular opinion, controls exist to maintain data accurately and securely. How does the concept justify hardware and software budget expenditures to support Data Base? Difficult question.

UTOPIA OR BOONDOGGLE?

Perspective is necessary. Data Base is here to stay. If only used as an access method, Data Base can provide a focal point for improving Data Processing. Data Base provides momentum; momentum for Data Processing to justify redesigning out-dated application systems, momentum to modernize procedures and standards. And in this capacity, the benefits are significant. Also, as with other major programs and expenditures, the industry will learn from the Data Base era.

But the key to future opinions of Data Base is expectations. If a company has presented Data Base as a focal point for developing online access, query capability, and standardization, then management will be well satisfied with the results. Utopia may not be the best word to characterize this state, but why not dramatize just a bit?

If, however, a corporation has been promised MIS, improved productivity, greater security and control, and reduced costs, then management may very well label the concept a boondoggle.

Historically, Data Processing has promised but not delivered. By establishing realistic expectations for Data Base, this unfortunate situation can be rectified.

PART V

CHAPTER ELEVEN DISCUSSION QUESTIONS

Is the approach to data base within an organization dependent on whether or not applications exist?

SUGGESTED READING

Sobczak, J. J., "A Data Base Story," Datamation, November 1977, pp. 139-150.

Kneitel, Arnold, "Dupont is Doing Things with MIS," Infosystems, February 1977, pp. 48-52.

Dearden, John, "MIS is a Mistake," Harvard Business Review, January-February 1972, Number 72105, pp. 121-130.

Nolan, Richard L., "Computer Data Bases: The Future is Now," Harvard Business Review, September-October 1973, pp. 98-114.

Dolotta, T. A., Et Al., Data Processing in 1980 - 1985, John Wiley & Sons, 1976.

BIBLIOGRAPHY

Nolan, Richard L., "Managing the Crises in Data Processing," Harvard Business Review, March-April 1979, pp. 115-126.

CHAPTER TWELVE

ECONOMICS OF MINIS*

Before presenting a cost comparison between minis and mainframes, general definitions of computer applications will be stated. Any definition which includes distributed processing can be challenged; however, less controversy is possible when the terms are vague. So, consider that corporations implement hardware and software for computer application in four modes:

        A.   Centralized

        B.   Distributed

        C.   Decentralized

        D.   Special Purpose (Turnkey)

A.   Centralized

Terminals are connected local or remote (communication controllers) to the central computer system. The majority of online "corporate" systems may be this type. They use the mainframe online system and data base language.

B.   Distributed

In the broad sense, Distributed Data Processing (DDP) or (Distributed Processing) is processing at a site with a means of bidirectional data transmission between the distributed site and the host site. The degree of control over files (data), programs, hardware and management issued may vary by application.

C.   Decentralized

Decentralized processing does not have an electronic link (transmission) between CPUs. Other elements that distinguish "decentralized" from "distributed" are the degree of control exercised by the user over the hardware, software and data at the remote site. Decentralized sites are more autonomous in nature and could be separate entities of the corporation.

Figure 12.1 (on the following page) graphically shows the first three application modes. With a distributed system, external communication services link multiple CPU's. As shown, terminals may be local or remote in all three modes

---

* Adapted from Johnson, <u>Mini or Mainframe</u>, pp. 59-60.

A. CENTRALIZED

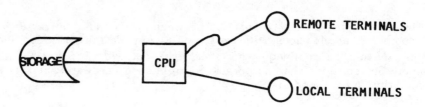

B. DISTRIBUTED

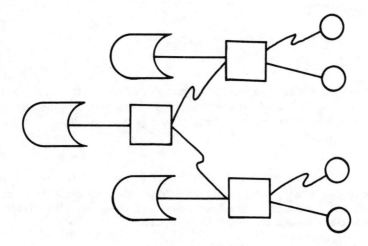

C. DECENTRALIZED

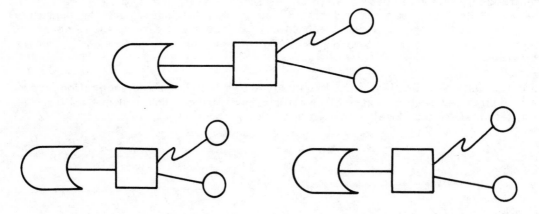

Figure 12.1 Centralized, Distributed, Decentralized

D. Special Purpose (Turnkey)

Special purpose systems are independent units of computing power, and devices not normally connected to a central site. They are used for a special purpose - usually not a general business application.

In the analysis which follows, centralized hardware versus distributed hardware is the issue. Decentralized and special purpose applications were included for definitional purposes.

THE ANALYSIS

Analyzing the cost of minis versus mainframes is a difficult task. There are two central issues - cost of processing and cost of communications.

Cost of Processing Between Centralized and Distributed

Does the processing power of one large computer exceed the processing power of ten smaller computers? This is the classic example of economies of scale. However, when comparing computers, it is impossible to perform a fair economic comparison.

Mini vendors have proposed the philosophy that a wise economic decision is to offload unnecessary processing from the mainframe. This logic implies that the law of economies of scale does not apply to computer processors. How is this argument substantiated? Since most computer centers have a standard costing technique for mainframe resources, the natural analysis is to compare the mini purchase price with the significant problems with this comparison:

1. Costs are not available for the mini.

2. Funny money (unused resources) is not the same as real, out-of-pocket expense.

Standard costing techniques for a mainframe generally include support costs for operating and maintaining the computer. The obvious expenses are floor space, heating and air conditioning, equipment rental, salary of operations, paper purchases, maintenance rental, salary of software personnel, etc.

Assuming the method of allocating costs is reasonable, it is important to illustrate what services these expenses provide:

1. Hardware conversions
2. Hardware maintenance
3. Software upgrades (operating systems, new compilers, optimizers, faster sorts)
4. Software maintenance
5. Operations support
6. Standardization (procedures, standards, and controls).

What are these costs for minis? Who knows? Using the purchase price of a mini is certainly not fair. Mini decisions are not based on economics - there are simply too many unknowns and intangibles.

The concept of funny money (value of unused capacity) which is implied with a standard costing technique is also a tough issue. The concept is not simple. Mainframe capacity comes in various forms - channels, disks, memory, CPU expansion, etc. A straightforward analysis of delaying the purchase of a mainframe is seldom the case. Thus, for these two reasons, it is not possible to fairly compare minis and mainframes on an economic basis.

What will happen if a comparison is made anyway? Of course, it depends on who is making the comparison. But nine times out of ten, the mini will win. Consider an online system with the characteristics shown below:

	Mini	Mainframe (IBM 168)
Price	$70,000	$3,000,000
Transaction/Day	5,000	150,000
Transaction/Year	1,300,000	39,000,000
$/Transactions	0.0538	0.0769
Mini Equivalents:		
On Volume	1	30
On Cost	1	43

If not on economics, on what would you base the decision?

Decisions to use minis in the "local" environment are based on five noneconomic factors. After presenting each reason, the pro and con logic will be briefly discussed.

1.   Principle of Decentralization

    a.   In the article "Is Decentralization Inevitable?" Wanger, F. V. (Datamation, November 1976 p. 97), a principle of decentralization is stated:

> If an organization group, smaller than
> 30 people, requires computer assistance,
> it is better for the total enterprise
> that those people have exclusive use of
> their own computer, provided that the
> computer, big enough to do the job
> properly, will be loaded to over 10%
> capacity.

    b.   This principle is labeled incorrectly. It should be titled, "The principle of computer power." The fact that a group of twenty to thirty individuals can improve productivity by using computer capabilities is independent of the size of computer. The benefits to the group would also be realized via CRTs to the mainframe. Actually, more software support (in the form of timesharing) is available on the larger equipment; for example, IBM's TSO or VSPC (Virtual Storage Personal Computing).

2.   User Control

  a.   A dedicated computer assures control of priorities. The user is not at the mercy of corporate preferences. When he wants to do his own thing, he can.

  b.   There are two points to be made. First, priorities and scheduling are not unique to large computers. Multiple applications on a mini can produce the same problem only at a local level. Second, is it in the corporation's best interests to allow individual users "free" use of computers, or should some control be exercised? After all, based on one definition of a mini (expense which can be included in a department or division budget), the corporate expense could easily grow out of control.

3.   Response Time/Reliability (Service)

  a.   Fast, consistent response is available on minis since the computer is dedicated to a few applications and overhead is minimal.

  Line delays and central site contention are two reasons for designing a distributed system. Remote response time from a central site is two to three seconds at a minimum. Many applications require one second response; for example, on data input the productivity may dramatically be reduced as response time increases. Also, distributed applications do not compete with other corporate priorities on the central computer. Thus, response time can be managed by the users in their area of responsibility.

  b.   If the central computer has poor response time or is down for extended periods, it may be time to reassess the equipment and/or data processing management. However, this is one of the strongest arguments for distributed equipment. Reliability of minis can be high, especially if the application is straightforward.

4.   Smaller Investment

  a.   A $40,000 down investment for a mini is much easier to justify than a $3 million mainframe. Especially if the company has a cash flow problem.

  b.   Difficult to argue if in financial difficulty. However, long-range planning is important. If ten minicomputers are possible over the next three years, the cash outlay might range from $200,000 to $1,000,000. And, again, the equipment per se is only a portion of the expense.

5.   Experiment

  a.   Companies have justified minis strictly on a research basis. There is nothing better than direct experience to help decide future direction.

  b.   Good point, but after equipment is installed, it is difficult to uninstall.

6.   Communication Costs

  a.   In certain situations, communications cost could be the deciding factor on a given application. An integral part of communication cost is the concept of local versus corporate data. If 90 percent of the data accessed is only needed on a local basis, it may be logical to store and update on local hardware instead of transmitting all the data to central hardware.

b.   Remote CRTs connected to the mainframe are also an alternative for applications. Analysis of communication costs is a specialty by itself. It is beyond the scope of this chapter to explore the many options.

CONCLUSION

Placing more computing power in the hands of corporate users can be accomplished via centralized, distributed, or decentralized equipment. A corporation that follows the minis trend without careful thought to the future could end up spending excessive resources for a given level of computer support. No one really knows which provides the overall economic advantage. It does appear that the benefits supporting minis have been overstated. Will the enthusiasm for minis die in the 1980s?

PART V

CHAPTER TWELVE DISCUSSION QUESTIONS

1.   What are the main reasons for the rapid spread of minis?

2.   Is it more economical to run seventy-five minis or two mainframes?

3.   How do communication costs impact the mini/mainframe decision?

SUGGESTED READING

Champine, G. A., "Six Approaches to Distributed Data Bases," Datamation, May 1977, pp. 69-72.

BIBLIOGRAPHY

Johnson, J. R., "Mini or Mainframe? An Online Question," Infosystems, April 1977, pp. 59-60.

Wagner, F. V., "Is Decentralization Inevitable?" Datamation, November 1976, pp. 86-97.

CHAPTER THIRTEEN

THE ULTIMATE MINI

For sale: The Ultimate 1, a computer which is considerably more powerful than IBM's 3033 for a total cost of $1,000. Please reference Figure 13.1 for the specifications. Briefly, the hardware circuitry is redundant, IBM software is supported, and the complete system is portable. Plus the limit on secondary storage is in the one trillion byte range. Of course, each 1 billion bytes is $100.

The salesperson is here taking orders. How many Ultimate minis will you buy - one, two, ten, fifty? As president of a major manufacturing company with 10,000 employees, you are aware of the endless demand for DP services. Each major division has at one time or another complained about existing DP response. In many cases, mini computers have been approved for specific applications, and a definite trend toward distributed processing is in progress. The philosophy that DP is the second business of all companies is almost a reality in your organization. The Ultimate mini sounds like the solution.

Thus, you ask all division managers to propose how one or more of the Ultimate mini computers would be used in their divisions. Briefly, selected responses are summarized as follows:

SELECTED RESPONSES

Data Processing

First, the division would reduce its hardware budget by $400,000/year by replacing the existing two IBM 370 158s with the Ultimate mini. Since CPU utilization was over 80 percent at times, an upgrade had already been proposed. Second, the programming staff has proven the personnel productivity potential of online compiles and debugging software. Unlimited hardware availability would enable each individual to have his or her own CRT. Third, the word processing center was having a difficult time justifying text editing and online storage space for corporate users; by having the Ultimate 1, the project could be expanded rapidly. And last, the capacity of the Ultimate 1 would allow the division to proceed on the corporate data base project which management had been reluctant to approve because of the potential CPU requirements.

Manufacturing

The CPUs residing in each of five manufacturing plants had been plagued with response time and disk capacity limitations. Also, there was a need for additional CRTs. An Ultimate 1 was requested for each plant.

Research

The Research division used the facilities of the central computer, but also had purchased three different minis for miscellaneous computational jobs. An Ultimate 1 would consolidate the hardware and provide extra capacity for manipulating large volume data bases.

1. CPU: Dual CPUs with 64K buffers (redundant design)
                            Cycle time = 1 nsec
                            Power supply = 110 volt with battery backup
                            Channels allowed = 50 max
                            Space requirements = 2 cubic feet
                            Weight = 1 lb.

2. Main Memory: 320 million bytes
                            Space requirements = 1 cubic foot

3. Secondary Storage: 1 billion byte increments @ $100 each
                            Space requirements = 3 cubic feet

4. Channels: Micro-code plug-ins, all I/O devices supported
                            (OCR, MICR, etc.): 50 channels @ 500K bps

5. Software: Runs IBM 370 operating systems, utilities and
                            compilers

6. Vendor Support: Excellent, backup equipment maintained on site
                            by vendor

7. CRTs: New compact version, cost $20

8. Printer: 15000 LPM laser; cost $375

9. Delivery Time: Immediate

10. Typical Business
    Configuration
    Purchase Price:

                    CPU, Buffers & Main Memory   = $100
                    Channels (3)   =   25
                    Secondary Memory   =   100
                    Printer (1)   =   375
                    CRT's (20)   =   400
                                                            ____

                            TOTAL $1,000

Figure 13.1 New Product Announcement

Marketing

This division could utilize portable CRTs for inquiry on inventory and customer sales. However, even with the Ultimate 1, the payback is marginal, since communication costs provide the real barrier.

Finance

The Financial division had developed the strongest analyst group in the company. Having designed the specifications for an integrated and sophisticated cost accounting system, the division was eager to proceed. Hardware constraints and programmer availability were hindering progress. If the Ultimate 1 were available, the division could justify a programming staff and implement the system on their own.

In addition to the above support for the Ultimate 1, one of your managers recently attended a seminar on the automated office which stressed company communication via CRTs. This is another application which might improve productivity.

Thus, your decision is to purchase fifty Ultimate 1 micro computers, or about one for every two hundred individuals. The price is right, and the extra capacity will provide for future growth.

WHAT HAPPENS?

Over the next year, most of your time and energy has been devoted to European business ventures. However, these issues have been resolved and it is now time to review the status of the Ultimate 1 within the corporation. Your $50,000 computer investment in the Ultimate 1 should have made considerable impact on the corporation. Thus, each division manager has been asked to present the budget and productivity improvement resulting from the purchase of their Ultimate 1s.

Data Processing

The first division reviewed was Data Processing. It is comforting to know that the hardware conversion project to the Ultimate 1 required one month and was completed on schedule. The hardware budget declined in excess of $400,000. Run times for the major applications were 10 percent of previous times. In Computer Operations, tape and disk mounters were eliminated through the use of secondary core storage.

The programming staff was delighted with Ultimate 1. Online editing, compile, and debug facilities improved, and further gains were anticipated when guidelines for programmers keying programs from CRTs were established.

Users of word processing capabilities praised the advent of the Ultimate 1. All secretaries were provided with CRTs and printers. Typing corrections on correspondence and documentation were no longer time-consuming.

The analysts required on the integrated data base system had doubled in number to a total of fifty persons. The complexity of the project was much greater than anticipated. User department personnel were spending considerable time defining the functional specifications of the MIS. When the value of data items was in doubt, the logic dictated inclusion since the cost was minimal. This was the first budget overrun encountered, but it was not viewed as adverse, since the potential benefits of an integrated system were so significant.

Also, the MIS project which links forecasting and long range facilities/resource allocation was in the initial investigation stage. Since hardware constraints were minimal, the manpower resources for design and programming were the limiting factors.

Manufacturing

The Ultimate 1 proved far superior to previous hardware. CRT expansion resulted in better information flow via increased online access.

Research

The hardware consolidation of computing power was a success. The division's major task was developing a relational type access method for retrieving huge volumes of historical sales data. Software development activities were not typically performed in this division, but the interest was so high management decided to pursue the project. The division was proceeding to hire fifteen analysts.

Finance

The division's first major project was struggling. The analyst staff requested sophisticated processing capabilities, and the twenty programming personnel had difficulty developing the complex logic. Management decided to proceed with only one phase of the project rather than the complete system.

Not all managers accepted the concept of communication via CRTs. However, the group using this capability were strong supporters of the concept. If everyone were persuaded to rely on the CRTs, they should prove even more effective.

You now sit back and reflect on the impact fifty Ultimate 1 computers have had on your corporation. There certainly is activity.

Hardware costs are down but you're not sure all the software development efforts will produce productive results. Have divisions overacted? Are they attacking marginal payback projects? How has the Ultimate 1 improved corporate profits?

THE POTENTIAL

The above example has set the stage for a more general discussion on the issue of productivity and the computer. The key question, assuming unlimited hardware, is the productivity of potential applications. What will people do with virtually unlimited computer power? For years the literature has highlighted one successful industry application after another. Examples include the following:

> Airline reservation systems
> Criminal data systems
> Online tracking systems
> Scheduling systems

The question is, how much potential is left. Or, a more probing question - what is the rate of return (productivity increase) of the applications? It is possible to classify corporate DP functions into five general applications, and they are explained below.

Basic Business Applications

These are the bread and butter applications which replace manual activities and are justified by personnel reductions. Examples are order processing, materials control, manufacturing scheduling, and accounting. For small ($50-100 million annual sales) corporations, generalized software on turnkey systems may satisfy the requirement.

Complex Business Applications

Those applications which involve complex software development may not cut costs directly, but rather have a probability of generating profit. Simulations, online access, and management information systems are examples of these applications.

Turnkey Applications

These applications require specialized processing; however, the processing is common among organizations. Examples of specific business functions are climate control, typesetting, and Watts box control or message switching. Turnkey mini/micro computer systems are appropriate for these applications, and future developments will result in the industrial robot.

Word Processing Applications

This general topic covers the following: text editing (typing corrections, reformation, word search), simple processing, sorting, indexing (local record storage and retrieval) and automated (electronic) mail distribution and printing.

FOUR TYPES OF PRODUCTIVITY

Before relating how the applications impact productivity, one other definitional task remains - defining the four types of productivity:

> Administrative
> Marketing
> Product
> Physical

Productivity can be improved in two ways: 1) Performing a function with fewer resources, or 2) Performing a function more effectively; i.e., producing a better product. Within a business, all productivity improvements are not equivalent. Computers, via applications, impact cost and/or profits in the following ways:

Reducing Administrative Costs

The basic systems provide the prime example. However, word processing and turnkey applications are also in this category.

Improving Product Marketing

Example: Timely sales data, demographic data, and customer service response. Both basic and complex systems provide this type of productivity improvement.

Improving the Product Itself

Applications in this category are isolated by industry and are not widespread. Take, for example, designing automobile frames using graphic terminals. Complex systems apply in this situation.

Performing Physical Work

Probably the greatest potential impact is in this category. Numerically controlled machines illustrate the concept. Automating other labor-intensive tasks may be slowed by unions, but eventually, robot-type machines will win the battle. Turnkey applications will provide this form of productivity to the corporation.

APPLICATION IMPACT

Figure 13.2 predicts the impact applications will have on productivity. The impact varies depending on the environment. Since computer power has been available historically in major corporations but not in small business, the small business environment is considered separately. Now, what does the chart say?

Environment

	Application	Corporate DP	Small Business
1.	Basic	L	H
2.	Complex	L	L
3.	Turnkey	H	H
4.	Word Processing	M	L-M

L = Low impact on productivity

M = Medium impact on productivity

H = High impact on productivity

Figure 13.2 Applications and Productivity

The basic application functions exist in the corporate DP environment; consequently, the potential for further improvements is low. Historically, these systems have been developed as necessitated by the business. Analyzing projects for an economic payback was the way DP got its start - the systems with the best rate of return were attacked first. Companies could not meet current production without this form of automation. Basic applications have the highest potential impact on small business. Probably 90 percent of the mini-success stories in periodicals are simply using the mini computers identical to the way big business used first and second generation computers in the 1960s. For example, paraphrasing one of the applications described by McCartney, "Small Business Systems: They're Everywhere" (Datamation October 1978, p. 92):

> The company recently purchased a computer and now has what is believed to be the first fully automated cemetery operation in the country. The machine performs all the usual business chores - accounting, payroll, and the like. It also monitors the organization's nursery operation, enabling the company to determine which types of plants and shrubs are selling the best and what inventory has to be replenished. Additionally, the system generates daily routing schedules for the lawn care service that tends Moriah's 100 acres. As in many businesses, the biggest concern is communicating with managers and keeping track of how effectively they're handling their operations. In total, the company employs 75 persons including a salesforce and managers for each of the major business segments (two funeral homes, two cemeteries, the flower shop, and nursery). The computer generates monthly reports from each of these groups, as well as commission statements for each salesperson. "It's made our entire operation much more efficient," the president says. Now if the computer could just be programmed to drive away ghosts. . .

The reason for the proliferation of minis is twofold: 1) They are obviously inexpensive, and 2) Turnkey software. These factors impose a modification on a popular adage: "There is no free lunch - except when a company can use a turnkey system on a mini." Thus, productivity potential exists for basic applications, but not for the entire corporate community.

Some might argue that complex applications have a high potential for productivity in the corporation. This question is debatable, but recording a "low," the author has taken the position that hardware technology is not the barrier to advanced management information systems. Rather, conflicting objectives and ownership of data are the limitations to complex systems (ref. Chapter Eleven - Data Base). Also, valuable profit generating systems exist today; for example, online airline reservation systems. In other words, the 1979-1980 technology is capable and has supported sophisticated systems for corporations with profitable applications. Other applications exist, but the resulting productivity improvement will be considerably less.

Similar logic applies to small business. In addition, small business will not have financial resources to support analyst and programming staffs required to develop complex systems. On the other hand, turnkey applications have high potential for both environments.

Human effort is generally directly replaced through the application of minis to special activities. To illustrate, consider a turnkey naval application. On a ship, a log of activities must be maintained recording course, speed, sea state, etc. Rather than logging these activities, a micro computer and keyboard with appropriate function buttons would vastly simplify this activity. Also, industrial robots, which are classified as turnkey systems, will eventually impact productivity dramatically.

Word processing applications have a greater potential impact on corporations than small businesses, because communications problems are more significant when interfaces increase. Since the productivity is in administration, the potential is rated medium and not high for corporations. Justifying word processing equipment based on clerical savings is a difficult task. Improvements exist, but the potential is limited. The benefits of an automated office (electronic distribution of memos, letters) can be significant in situations where timely communications have not been resolved satisfactorily by other means (typing pool, telephone, meetings). In addition to disseminating one-time communication, the problem of mass updating manuals and standards may be resolved. For example, one hundred standards manuals may reside in ten remote physical locations. If the material were online and updated via one source, productivity would indirectly improve.

MANAGEMENT ISSUES

The mental exercise of predicting the utilization of an Ultimate 1 computer produces an interesting corporate scenario. The thought process centers on applications and their impact on productivity.

Historically, hardware costs have provided an inherent "Cost Control Mechanism" for managing the growth of DP applications. Over the past five years, the lower cost of mini computers has de-emphasized hardware purchases as a control mechanism. The management emphasis has been in two areas: 1) Assuring standard interfaces among equipment, and 2) Centralized definition of common data. However, when hardware costs are virtually eliminated, the emerging problem is controlling software development.

Consider multiple divisions within a corporation all embarking on Stage II growth cycles in regard to software development. The people resources are spread over many budgets, and consequently, they are neither visible nor easily managed. An out-of-control situation may result.

How does management control development of complex software projects which may have no payback to the company? Two suggestions are offered. First, develop a framework for classifying application productivity. When applications are proposed, usually via hardware purchases, assess the application for its impact on productivity in relation to software complexity. In-house development of complex systems is the main concern (as illustrated in the scenario for the DP, Research, and Finance Divisions).

Second, a formal method of monitoring software staffing should be established. It is easy to conceal mini purchases in budgets and easier to conceal software (analysts and programming) personnel.

Having unlimited hardware resources emphasizes the requirement for a new control mechanism in data processing. This control is focused on the personnel required to develop systems. If control is not exercised, costs will exceed benefits. Advanced planning is required to control the ultimate mini.

PART V

CHAPTER THIRTEEN DISCUSSION QUESTIONS

1. When hardware is no longer a consideration, what will be the issue?

2. Do all types of applications have the same impact on productivity?

SUGGESTED READING

Martin, James, <u>The Wired Society</u>, Prentice-Hall, Inc., 1978.

BIBLIOGRAPHY

McCartney, Layton, "Small Business Systems: They're Everywhere," <u>Datamation</u>, October 1978, pp. 91-93.

CHAPTER FOURTEEN

PRODUCTIVITY AND THE ORGANIZATION*

THE CHANGING DP ORGANIZATION

Just as nature has a "life cycle," so the DP organization has a cycle in which functions performed in one organization are terminated only to produce growth and expansion in other organizations. This section describes the life cycle of data processing, and shows that functions of the DP organization, as it existed between 1950 and 1960, will be eliminated by 1985, only to emerge in other areas - namely, user departments.

The responsibilities of the DP organization have been changing over the years. User departments now perform tasks traditionally done by the DP department. This shifting of responsibilities will continue for two important reasons: 1) new technological advancements encourage such shifts, and 2) human nature - people desire to control factors that influence their performance, in this case, DP systems.

To provide a perspective for the future, it is appropriate to start by discussing how both technology and human nature have historically influenced the DP organization. Then in Section 14.2 barriers to productivity will be discussed.

14.1 Organizational Influences

1950 - 1960

First, what functions did the DP organization perform in the 1950 - 60 era? (listed in Figure 14.1). The initial applications on the computer were the systems such as accounting and payroll which were previously supported by electronic accounting machines. Elimination of repetitive manual work was the justification for the newly acquired tool.

To the users, computers were unknown, complex technical machines. Even programmer/analysts did not understand the complete technical aspects of the machine, and certainly did not understand fully the commercial customers' information processing needs.

Users expressed their mistrust of the computer by maintaining files long after the data had been placed on the computer. The control for systems design was in the DP department. Systems were implemented by programmer/analysts, with part-time, often reluctant, user participation. The DP department also selected and maintained the computer hardware.

1960 - 1970

In this era, the concept of project management teams to design DP systems emerged and became a way of life. The project manager was in the DP organization. User personnel, however, were assigned to the project on a full-time basis. This active user participation in design and implementation of DP projects is the dominant reason that today, individuals outside of data processing are well acquainted with the capabilities of computers in the business world. Of course, more extensive education in universities and just plain additional exposure to computers have also contributed to general knowledge of the computer's capabilities.

---

* Adapted from Johnson, The Changing D.P. Organization, pp. 81-85.

ERA	TECHNOLOGY/CONTROL FACTORS		FUNCTIONS OF USER DEPARTMENTS		FUNCTIONS OF DP DEPARTMENTS	
1950-60	1.	Computers are new tools	1.	Part-time participation on design of DP systems	1.	Select and maintain hardware
	2.	Lack of understanding of computers	2.	Maintain data base	2.	Control the design effort
					3.	Full-time participation on project teams
					4.	Employ programmer/analysts
1960-70	1.	Proliferation of technology	1.	Full-time participation on project teams	1.	Select and maintain hardware
	2.	Project teams emerge			2.	Control the design effort
					3.	Full-time participation on project teams
					4.	Employ analysts
					5.	Employ programmers
					6.	Maintain data base
1970-75	1.	MIS	1.	Control of project team	1.	Select and maintain hardware
	2.	Teleprocessing	2.	Full-time participation on project teams	2.	Full-time participation on project teams
	3.	Better understanding of computer usage			3.	Employ analysts
					4.	Employ programmers
					5.	Maintain data base
1975-85	1.	Distributed processing	1.	Control of project team	1.	Select and maintain hardware
	2.	Corporate data base	2.	Full-time participation on project teams	2.	Part-time participation on design
	3.	High-level language	3.	Employ analysts	3.	Employ programmers
			4.	Limited programming	4.	Maintain data base
1985-95	1.	High-level application software for mini-computers	1.	Select and maintain hardware	1.	Part-time participation on design
			2.	Control the design effort	2.	Maintain data base
			3.	Full-time participation on project teams		
			4.	Employ programmer/ analysts		

TABLE 14.1 The Life Cycle of Data Processing

Another concept evolved during this era. With the proliferation of new software (operating systems, application languages, utilities) and hardware (storage devices such as discs and tapes, input devices like key-to-disk systems, output forms such as microfilm), it became a full-time job just to keep current in DP technology. It was also becoming obvious that greater emphasis had to be placed on learning business functions in order to design a business system. Thus, one man was required to know too much.

A separation of functions offered a solution to the problem, and programmer/analysts were thus replaced by programmers and analysts. Analysts specialized in understanding user functions, and programmers specialized in programming. Program run write-ups became the means of communication between analysts and programmers.

1970 - 1975

During the early 1970 time frame, most organizations have studied some form of MIS (Management Information System). MIS is defined as a system, usually complex, which converts raw data into valuable management information. Examples of MIS applications include forecasting, automatic scheduling, exception reporting, and programmed decision rules. Progress in this area of computer usage has been judged essential to an organization's existence. Those companies not profiting from the huge potential payoff may simply not stay competitive.

The organization of project teams developing MIS has changed only slightly, but very significantly, during the 1970-75 era. The user has now become the project manager. This has happened for three reasons. First, user acceptance of designs for computer systems has in the past been a problem, and this problem comes closer to resolution if the user-manager has done the design. Second, for users, the unknown is becoming known: the mystery of what computers can do is gradually disappearing. And third, the human tendency to control those things required to perform one's job has become a major factor - users now desire to manage as well as design the project effort.

Technical advances in this era have also revolved around teleprocessing. Systems are designed to provide online retrieval validation and updating of data files. People in many company departments have direct access to data bases.

Having been exposed to online systems and MIS, users are becoming more demanding of their DP systems.

1975 - 1985

Moving into the current period brings some significant changes. Users now have experience in the design and implementation of major systems. Staff functions in user areas, such as scheduling, manufacturing control, finance, and purchasing have grown in size. Since many users who participated in designing DP systems are now back in their home departments, the various user areas have "systems" people in their organization.

In effect, the analyst (the former DP analyst) now reports to a user manager. And the DP organization is relieved of the design responsibility for DP systems, which now rests with the user.

The popular concept of the era are corporate data bases and distributed processing. (On the surface, having a corporate data base seems to contradict the trend toward letting the user departments design their own DP systems. This apparent contradiction is resolved by letting the user department DP analyst work with the logical relationships of data, while having the DP department maintain the data base software which handles the computer relationships.) Distributed processing lends itself to centralized control, since most of the programming is done in macro or assembler languages. However, part of the hardware is physically located with the user - a trend which will continue.

During this era, individuals from user departments write their own programs. Basic retrieval (extract, sort, and list) with a high-level language, either online or batch processing, is the main purpose of these programs. The need for such a tool, retrieval, will vary from application to application; however, there is no way that a system can be designed to meet all possible current and future variations that will occur. Thus users find the retrieval capability an excellent tool for solving both one-time and periodic problems. They also laud the convenience of the process, because they no longer have to wait weeks for the DP department to process their requests, since they now process them themselves.

In short, during this era, users are experiencing for the first time the advantages of having their own programming staff, whatever its size.

1985 - 1995

Distributed processing will by now have become very popular. Computer manufacturers will have expended most of their resources over a number of years, developing minicomputer technology. High level programming languages will be application oriented. Users will now be able to design DP systems on their own minicomputers with their own personnel. The hardware will be physically located in user areas.

The job functions of analysts and programmers will also have changed. User departments will once again combine the job classification of analyst and programmer into one position: programmer/analyst. They will reason that higher level programming is so straightforward that it is not beyond the capabilities of one man to know both the business functions of the company and the language.

An interesting phenomenon will have occurred: responsibilities that existed in the 1950-60 era for major company departments and those for the DP department will have been exchanged. DP personnel will participate in system design, but only on a part-time basis. The responsibility for maintaining the corporate data base will have shifted from the user organization to the data processing organization. Users will now be the ones to select and maintain hardware, to control the design effort, and to employ programmer/analysts.

The factors influencing this almost complete shift in responsibilities between the user departments and the DP department will be primarily the advances in technology which will make such a shift possible, and the ever present variable of human nature, which manifests itself in the desire for control of the systems one works with.

Thus, a life cycle similar to that found in nature also exists in the data processing world. The elimination of the DP organization as it existed in the 1950-60 time frame will have been accomplished by 1985, but its functions will have found new life in other (namely, user) organizations.

14.2 BARRIERS TO PRODUCTIVITY

Based on the organization changes explained in the previous section, productivity barriers during the last two periods (1975-85 and 1985-95) are now discussed for both the user and DP organizations.

Bureaucracy, Complexity & Job Enrichment (DP 1975-85)

Webster defines the term bureaucratic as "A system of administration marked by red tape." Complexities in DP lead to specialization, and specialization leads to additional interfaces. Also, size leads to detailed controls, procedures, and additional paperwork. Thus, both complexity and size contribute to a bureaucratic DP organization.

Bureaucracy results in lack of responsiveness. Today, DP organizations have become bureaucratic, not because of poor management, but because of the complexity of hardware, software, and application systems. This complexity has produced specialization, and in some cases, over-specialization. What specialists exist in this era?

1. Operating system specialists
2. Online specialists
3. Auditing specialists
4. Equipment specialists
5. JCL experts
6. Data base administrators
7. System test experts
8. Documentation specialists
9. Training specialists
10. Performance monitoring specialists

In addition to the specialists, our large complex organizations require procedures - procedures for control, security, documentation, and so forth. Most large organizations have DP standard procedure books of more than 200 pages.

Another aspect of bureaucracy is reflected in the tasks required to make a small programming change to an existing system. Prior to bureaucracy, a programmer made the change, inserted it in production, and made himself available in case it blew up.

Today, in our more bureaucratic environment, the procedure is quite different. 1) The program must be changed on the test library; 2) The change must be tested; 3) A turnover meeting is required to inform other DP departments that a change is planned; 4) The documentation package must be modified; 5) The test version is used in production mode, and if successful, 6) The test version is compiled for the production library. This simple change that may have required four hours, five to ten years ago, now may require three to four mandays and two weeks elapsed time.

This is not meant to imply that these steps are not required today. After all, systems may be interrelated, and production problems on one system can change the entire production schedule. However, the central point is that overspecialization reduces personnel motivation within DP. There is less satisfaction in the work because jobs are very specific. Everyone performs efficiently, but personnel do not necessarily feel responsible for the success of the project. Ideally, a programmer's response to the question "What are you building?" would be, "A system to improve the profits of the corporation by providing more timely information to the sales force."

This is the age-old issue of job enrichment. Unfortunately, good solutions to the problem are difficult to define. Fortunately, in the next era of organizational development (1985-95), technological changes should reduce the magnitude of the problem; i.e., distributed hardware will not be as complex, and more important, software will be of a higher level.

The Pseudo User (1975-85)

A pseudo user is defined as follows:

1. He represents the real user (operating management).

2. He is expected to have a close rapport with the real user and speak for him on many design questions.

3. He has limited DP design knowledge since the assignment is only a stepping stone, or a tentative learning period prior to his becoming a real user.

4. He does not want to look ignorant to either the DP personnel or the real user; thus, his analysis is based on how he thinks a particular function is performed, rather than on research.

5. He generally produces poor system specifications.

This impediment to productivity is a difficult issue. Design sign-offs, prototype systems, and communication are the tools for prevention.

Career Paths (1985-95)

Another ramification of the job enrichment productivity barrier is limited career paths. During the 1975-85 era, opportunities for transferring to user organizations were plentiful, since DP knowledge was still in short supply. However, as corporate DP personnel became even more specialized in the complexities of the giant mainframe, and as users develop knowledge in DP, the career path out of DP will narrow.

This presents only a psychological problem since it will reverse a trend established by chance. But actually, DP will become like other professions (for example, engineering), in that career opportunities outside the profession will be limited.

User Portfolio Selection (1985-95)

When users manage the entire DP function on a distributed basis during the 1985-95 era, productivity may be adversely impacted by a poor selection of applications.

Historically, the Data Processing division has acted as a reviewing body for DP projects. This review is healthy because it provides consistent guidelines for all divisions.

But each division manager has unique information requirements based on his management style or approach to his job. Some managers insist on detailed reports while others prefer summary level information. When the system designer's boss is defining the system, there is a strong tendency to provide exactly what is asked for rather than to define the "real" information needs based on the purpose of the system. Analogously, there is a strong tendency to devote the majority of resources to applications judged important by the "current" manager in charge. Not that division managers shouldn't have the final say in what is and isn't important, but arbitrary decisions should be avoided in the distributed environment.

Thus, a reviewing body is essential. Two logical organizations are possible - corporate DP or Internal Audit. Establish procedures so arbitrary decisions are not made within your company. Budget accountability is not adequate. It is important to have the costs and benefits of every feasibility study reviewed by "outsiders" for all projects.

PART V

CHAPTER FOURTEEN DISCUSSION QUESTIONS

SECTION

14.1   1.   Technology is an obvious force directing organizational change. What are some others?

14.2   2.   Why discuss future barriers to productivity?

SUGGESTED READING

Dolotia, T. A., et al, <u>Data Processing in 1980-85</u>, John Wiley & Sons, 1976.

BIBLIOGRAPHY

Johnson, J. R., "The Changing D.P. Organization", <u>Datamation</u>, January, 1975, pp. 81-85.

CHAPTER 15

EPILOG

The following quote is from the front page of <u>Computerworld</u> (Dec. 24, 1979):

> "IBM will begin customer shipments of its System/38 small business computer sometime in July, nearly a year after its originally scheduled release date, the company announced last week."

What is the reason for this one-year delay? Is it possible that IBM has overlooked some of the basic management productivity techniques? On the System/38 project, did they:

1. Estimate the project mandays using a macro LOC approach;

2. Provide for adequate test time;

3. Allow online compile and debug;

4. Use meaningful, nonbureaucratic, project control to manage the work;

5. Estimate the total project rather than dividing the project into ten phases and estimating each phase when the previous phase is completed;

6. Define appropriate standards;

7. Assure that the project managers had project responsibility rather than DP auditors;

8. Make the correct design decisions concerning the data base access methods capabilities?

The answers to these questions may never be made public, but the year delay does emphasize the difficulty, even for IBM, of managing a large DP effort.

As supported by the previous fourteen chapters, managing for productivity is a vast subject. There is no one answer. The author is hopeful that the material in this book can be applied to improve performance in many organizations.

As we proceed through the 1980s, managing for productivity will continue as an integral function of DP management.

APPENDIX 1

MANDAY DEFINITIONS

The purpose of this Appendix is to clarify the definition of a manday. It is important that the division use consistent terminology when developing work plans, Gantt charts, and other time estimates.

I. DEFINITIONS

A. Time Reporting Hour

1. Definition: Hours loaded into time reporting system for historic record of time expended. Time reporting hours are the actual hours reported on a task.

2. Use: Planning and estimating for well defined tasks and Gantt charting. Time reporting hours are appropriate for smaller tasks.

B. Manday

1. Definition: Time in days to accomplish a task or project. Mandays include a 33 percent addition above time reporting hours for general and administrative activities. In other words, on the average, six time reporting hours equate to one eight hour day - a manday. Large segments of administrative time, such as vacation, should be considered separately when Gantting.

2. Use: To compute manpower costs, to draw Gantt charts, and to estimate scope at a macro level. Mandays are more appropriate for estimating larger tasks. They are macro, more general estimates than time reporting hours.

C. Elapsed Time (Weeks or Months)

1. Definition: Calendar time (vs. workdays) to complete a task. Overlapping tasks, vacations, and scheduling dependencies are considerations for estimating elapsed time.

2. Use: To estimate completion dates.

II. RELATIONSHIPS

6 Time Reporting Hours	=	1 manday
20 Mandays	=	1 manmonth
240 Mandays	=	1 manyear

III. GANTTS

Gantt charts can be drawn with either time reporting hours or mandays. If time reporting hours are used, they will total less than the available hours. However, if mandays are used and if all tasks are Gantted, workdays will total mandays assigned.

For example:

Gantt Individual A	Man Days	Week One	Two
Task 1	3	→	
Task 2	3	→	
Task 3	4	→	
	10		

Note that elapsed time exceeds mandays in each case, but ten mandays of tasks require ten elapsed days.

IV.   SUMMARY

When developing work plans, Gantt charts, program estimates, use one of the above definitions. Also, specify any other assumptions or variations.

APPENDIX 2

ANSWERS

PART I, Chapter One

Section One

1. LOC rates vary based on definitions - manhours, rules for counting LOC, nature of programming effort, and language.

2. LOC is not a good measure of "individual" programmer performance. The difficulty of the coding assignment, and more importantly, the quality of the code, are two factors which remain subjective. Progress has been made in the area of quality, but to date, pragmatic tools do not exist. On the other hand, LOC data should not be totally ignored. It should be one input to an individual's performance rating along with other inputs, which result from typical management tools such as work plan and Gantt charts.

3. This subject is addressed in Chapter Five. Briefly, LOC estimating at a macro level helps establish the scope of a project. If the scope of a project is under-estimated, many poor decisions result. Design or programming short-cuts produce an inefficient and unmaintainable product.

4. Definitely yes, discussion on productivity implies that individual productivity is the issue. The basic theme of this book indicates that there are multiple facets to productivity. In regard to LOC, more benefits result from using data for high level estimating than for individual performance. Personnel produce what they are expected to produce. If LOC is the only monitoring tool, human ingenuity will devise unlimited ways of generating code. At a macro level, when comparing one project to another, minor inconsistencies balance out based on the law of large numbers.

Section Two

5. Not very well. DP, even though a relatively young profession, does a better job than other disciplines. Also, significant research is being directed toward measurement of all aspects of DP productivity. Thus, DP will continue to improve productivity measures.

6. Yes, if performance does not have a direct relationship to pay, incentive is lacking. This does not mean that other forms of recognition are unimportant - they are. But pay is still the single best incentive, especially when group members perform similar activities in the same environment.

7. Since chance is the rule rather than the exception in the DP world, establishing an absolute scale for certain functions is not possible. The Operations environment presents fewer obstacles than the development/programming environment. Remember, there is nothing inherently "wrong" with relative rankings.

8. Performance reviews should be based on specific contributions. The question points out a basic conceptual issue when preparing reviews; i.e., start by listing

contributions - not individual talents. Talents may or may not apply during the review period.

9. Yes, formal reviews should be directly linked to salary increases which are generally annual. However, this does not imply that other forms of praise and recognition should be limited to formal reviews.

Section Three

10. Generally speaking, two years does appear to be a natural burnout period; however, no empirical evidence is offered to support this opinion. As with any average, there are circumstances where six months or three years is appropriate.

11. Short term lack of expertise on a given assignment is the main reason managers are reluctant to rotate individuals. Management must believe that stagnation will result if people are not presented with new challenges. (See Chapter Seven for other specific benefits of applying the burnout theory.)

12. a. Facilitates collecting appropriate data for decision on promotions and re-assignments.

    b. Allows individuals to state their interests, skills and preferences.

    c. Provides basis for manager's mid-year conversation with individual.

    d. Serves as a history of personal accomplishments.

13. One of two things, either the criteria defined do not reflect the real criteria, or the criteria should be weighed unequally. In this situation, you may want to correct the criteria to reflect your feelings.

PART I, Chapter 2

Section One

1. Circumstances in different organizations may negate some of the statements expressed. For example, shops without automated librarian software would, no doubt, legitimately justify a person to function as librarian. Also, the HIPO technique can be useful, but there are better techniques.

Section Two

2. The section takes a strong position to make a point; i.e., structured diagrams can be misused. As with any tool, use it if it is beneficial; but remember, by far the greatest tool is structured programming, so don't expect the same results when applying other techniques to different problems and other tasks.

3. The main reason other structured diagrams are recommended over HIPO is that the sequence of execution is inherent in the technique.

Section Three

4.   If the environment is commercial applications, and the definitions for L O C and time are similar to those presented, the results should be similar.

PART II, Chapter 3

1.   Not in the sense of individual or project productivity, but as it relates to management's selection of the appropriate projects. In other words, once 40-50 % of the resources have been committed, management is extremely reluctant to cancel the project. A better approach is to use high level estimating techniques (Chapter 5), and be more certain of the scope before starting design.

PART II, Chapter 4

1.   Cost factors could be emphasized more, but on software projects, mandays represent over 80 percent of the cost.

2.   No, if the project goes as scheduled, the information derived from monitoring project tasks is never utilized. On low risk projects, the effort devoted to project monitoring should not be overemphasized.

PART II, Chapter 5

1.   No, not directly. Each corporation must develop its own historic data base, based on their accepted assumptions. The data presented has value as an indirect comparison.

2.   When a project grows beyond a certain point, complexity increases at an increasing rate. The main reasons are additional software, logic, and people interfaces. It also implies that the programming phase on a small project is a larger percentage of the total project; i.e., the feasibility study, design, system test, and conversion phases comprise a relatively smaller part of the total project. Thus, a large and small project may have similar programming L O C rates but much different project L O C rates as illustrated by the 3 to 1 ratio.

3.   Definitely yes. They provide consistency within an organization. But remember, do not misuse them as performance measures.

PART II, Chapter 6

Section One

1.   Peer pressure is probably the best way to direct concentration to testing techniques. The feedback reports discussed will accomplish the task.

Section Two

2.   Yes, there would be little advantage for the functions of compiling, unit and system testing. However, other functions which facilitate data set manipulation, such as inquiry/list and build/change, are valuable on their own.

Section Four

3.   Testing metrics also provide justification for "good" turnaround. As discussed, test time availability can be directly related to the project's progress during system test.

PART III, Chapter 7

1.   Probably so, because the objectives defined for the manager are at macro or summary level, and are thus subject to less variations, although in both situations individual performance cannot be quantified 100 percent. A subject interpretation of the challenges and constraints is always necessary.

2.   To say that on the average a maintenance programmer can support 50,000 LOC is meaningful only as a guideline. Some systems, because of their link to changing business functions, may require a ratio of one person to 20,000 LOC.

PART III, Chapter 8

Section One

1.   No, and that is the main point, usually overlooked.

Section Two

2.   Good question, but also ambiguous. Many extract type languages are in use today, but progress in this area is slow. For example, developing a language for only financial applications is expensive and difficult. Think of the problem of standardization.

3.   All but the extreme diehards will admit Assembler is on its way out. Mini computers brought Assembler a brief breath of life, but high level languages are the future, even for minis.

Section Three

4.   Definitely not, applying basic management principles is advised (see Chapter Four).

Section Four

5.   Yes. Tuning projects are never wasted effort, unless, of course, hardware resources are available in excess.

Section Six

6.   First, people do not want to commit to dollarizing benefits when there is no way to prove or substantiate the estimate. Second, a procedure like the one presented is necessary.

Section Seven

7.   By having a noninvolved party review the report, obvious errors will be discovered.

PART IV, Chapter 9

Section One

1. Monitoring the source and frequency of unusual conditions provides management with an effective measurement tool. The number of UCRs indirectly and sometimes directly relates to the quality of service provided by the DP division. For example, if the number of abnormal terminations (per day) of the online network increases from two to three, a record of UCRs will provide a means of analyzing why. Also, a history of UCR performance provides a base for improvement.

2. The key to the answer is based on testing and conversion factors. If parallel passes are possible, five to ten UCRs might be considered good. For some unique systems, fifteen to twenty might be anticipated.

Section Two

3. As corporations become more and more dependent on computers, the consequences of losing the computer facility increase. Computer hardware reliability is not the issue. Disaster recovery by definition addresses long term outages - not temporary down time.

Section Three

4. Without a specific criterion, it is difficult to decide what is and is not appropriate for a standard. The extreme case would be to document every aspect of an individual's activity.

Section Five

5. Planning sessions that accomplish the following:

    a. Assure that all managers understand the division objectives

    b. Provide a forum to discuss mutual problems

    c. Establish a plan of action to resolve problems.

Section Seven

6. Yes and no. Auditors should have responsibility for defining system controls necessary for reliable audit trails and balancing. Auditors should not have scheduling, monitoring, or status reporting responsibilities - those are the province of the project manager.

Section Eight

7. The major conferences cover every aspect of data processing - software, application, mainframes, communication, minis, and peripheral devices. Interest must be focused on a subject to obtain specific knowledge.

PART IV, Chapter 10

1.   No, the benefits of a training department are best utilized by providing consistent training of basic skills. Advanced level training is usually on-the-job, but can be taught via seminars.

2.   Probably not, the ingredients which comprise human nature will not have changed by the year 2000.

PART V, Chapter 11

1.   Definitely. Existing systems provide complex constraints on data base progress. Design of ideal data structures is difficult, and when other contraints are present, the complexity is enormous. For example, for a company with three million LOC designed application by application, it may require 100-200 manyears to ideally redesign for data base.

PART V, Chapter 12

1.   First, an apparent cost/performance advantage. Second, inconsistent service from the central site - slow response time, late reports, computer nonavailability. Third, lack of programming resources from the central site. Users do not want to wait six months just to discuss their ideas.

2.   Difficult question to answer. The current trend toward minis supports the decision to go seventy-five minis. However, both approaches have worked successfully in different corporations, and more recently, problems associated with minis have surfaced (upgrading, maintenance, interfaces).

3.   Communication costs can have a dramatic impact on the mainframe/mini decision. Each organization must carefully assess the merits of the "distributed" approach.

PART V, Chapter 13

1.   First, managing the people resources devoted to developing and maintaining application systems. Second, implementing the applications with the greatest impact on corporate productivity.

2.   Definitely not. Each organization should define and classify productivity in its environment. Estimating intangible dollar benefits (Chapter 8) for potential applications is also a necessary part of the procedure.

PART V, Chapter 14

Section One

1.   Other forces directing organizational change are control of resources directly related to their functions, the bureaucracy of DP which results in lack of responsiveness, and the DP education or expertise of user personnel.

Section Two

2.   Discussing future barriers to productivity provides management time to plan control and motivational aspects in the future environment.

INDEX

INDEX

INDEX

INDEX